A Boy for All Seasons, but a Man...?

A Boy for All Seasons, but a Man...?

BOYS NEED A HERO'S JOURNEY TO
REACH VIRTUOUS MANHOOD

Thomas R. Caffrey

© 2018 Thomas R. Caffrey

All rights reserved. Printed in the United States of America. No part of this book may be reproduced in any manner whatsoever without written permission except in the case of brief quotations embodied in critical articles and reviews.

ISBN-13: 9780692561485 (Custom)
ISBN-10: 069256148X
LCCN: 2015919016
Library of Congress Control Number: 2015919016
Fp Publishing, West Creek, NJ

1. Memoir—United States—Self-Help. 2. Philosophy—Christianity—Catholicism.
3. Boys—Manhood—Commentary. 4. History—World. 4. Education—United States.
5. Traditional—United States.

For Kevin and Maureen:
My most noble purpose, my greatest meaning and joys;
the reason I know His agape love

also to
My parents, Joseph and Janice: for keeping their covenant, thereby giving witness
that it can be done

and
St Thomas More: for his devotion to faith, family and truth
from a well-formed conscience

and
Chris Tivenan: through it all, my friend of 55 years

Table of Contents

Introduction ································ xi

Chapter 1   The Beginning ························ 1
Chapter 2   It's a Boy! ···························· 6
Chapter 3   Peer Review ·························· 20
Chapter 4   Declaration of Independence ······· 25
Chapter 5   Multi-Cultural Manhood ············ 29
Chapter 6   Media *Does* Matter ················· 40
Chapter 7   The Dating Game ···················· 48
Chapter 8   Heroic Warriors, or Worriers? ····· 59
Chapter 9   Schooling Our Boys ················· 66
Chapter 10   Political Correctness: The New B.S. Degree ········· 83
Chapter 11   The Hard Knocks of Becoming Number One ········ 110
Chapter 12   The Birds and the Bees and the Boys ················ 121
Chapter 13   Have We Cause for Hope? ······················· 146
Chapter 14   Faith from Our Father, and His Son ············· 154
Chapter 15   The Transcendent More ························· 176

Postlude ·· 189
In Gratitude ····································· 191
About the Author ································ 193

"The Way"

The call is made from near and far
so how will you respond?
The choice you make will form your life
today and far beyond

But which direction should you take
and whose advice is true?
Decide you must, the journey waits
for no one else but you

The path is partly cleared by men
who've walked before your time,
the rest is up to you my son,
to manhood you must climb.

With each step you near the goal,
a purposeful mission,
but into Satan's lair you'll fall
when you give into sin.

Yet rise you must and carry on,
forgiven, you're restored
head True North for your manliness
to Jesus Christ our Lord.
TRC

Introduction

LIKE MOST MEN, I IMAGINE, I've long pondered what it means to "become a man," to "be a man," and to "achieve heroic manhood"—rather than just to become an adult male. It wasn't until my teenage years that I believed assertions such as one made by the Reverend Billy Sunday, who said, "you can't measure manhood with a tapeline around his biceps." But I eventually learned that those biceps, along with the rest of me, could be used virtuously—heroically—if I had both the will *and* the training. A girl becomes a woman simply by their passage into adulthood. Not so for boys. That's not to say that that passage into womanhood is easy for a girl, because history shows how difficult life has been, generally, for females around the world. The difference for boys has historically been the *public* tests they must pass as, for examples, provider and protector in order to earn the public *and* private honor that most greatly desire.

The movement from childhood to adulthood is never easy, because life is complicated and difficult. Of course, very often the reason for many of these difficulties is the dishonorable and immoral behavior of humans, and thereby pointing to the absence of virtue. Thinkers such as Plato and Aristotle (about whom more will be written later in this book) believed that the happy and fulfilled life is the greatest aspiration of moral behavior, and that only through developing the skills associated with the virtues can we attain that happiness. But today, too many of us—especially boys—are not receiving the guidance and training necessary to develop those skills, and virtue goes lacking.

In recent years my thinking about this was done in the context of having a son, centering on how I should raise him to become the best "man" possible; and by doing this help him to know that the real meaning and purpose in a man's life is to be a man *for others*. As Christians, he would have a rich stable of models for this way of life. His greatest test would be, as it was for me and is for all, how well he would fare as he moves away from home to face those aforementioned and inevitable challenges—especially in a culture that has steadily diminished and devalued traditional ideas surrounding morality, masculinity, gender, and, most certainly, virtuous manhood. When I became a father to Kevin I pondered this matter with some urgency, because I would be his main influence and because I was acutely aware of my own shortcomings and those of increasing numbers of boys.

This book will explore some of the history, research, and social changes pertaining to boys and their growth into manhood; tell stories of my boyhood experiences and those of my son; and give commentary with some challenges. I do not preach, as my falls from grace forbid that; but I hope to challenge and encourage the reader—and myself. Each chapter describes these changes in relation to a different aspect of a boy's life, such as play, education, sexuality, family, relationships and competition. Woven into all of them are the threads of faith, philosophy, mythology and literature, and in the context of the Hero's Journey motif. I hope it will tell how a father and his son were able to work together, in a whole family as well as in one that became broken, to help one become a virtuous man and the other a better one—in spite of cultural pressures and a father's imperfections.

Increasingly we find books, articles and commentary describing the decline of the American male, in the following examples:

The Trouble with Boys[1]
"Memo to Parents: Stop Coddling Your Kids"[2]
The End of Men[3]

---

1 Peg Tyre, *The Trouble with Boys*, (Harmony, 2009)
2 Dr. Keith Ablow, foxnews.com (January 11, 2012)
3 Hanna Rosin, *The End of Men*, (Riverhead Books, 2012)

"Are Fathers Necessary?"
Are Men Necessary?[4]
Is There Anything Good About Men?[5]

This is a phenomenon that will find its way into future history books. The emphasis is typically on lagging academic performance, decreasing drive for achievement and relationships, and men's struggle for identity, purpose and meaning as society shifts toward a new definition of manhood (if that word will still be allowed): one that does not suggest the traditional "hero."

Although some of this criticism is hyperbole, there is much to concern us. It is curious and troubling that so many of today's adult males have not only allowed this decline to occur, but also have knowingly contributed to it as well. This change is in stark contrast with the long and multi-cultural traditions of men guiding boys into manhood, which this book will explore.

In the past, it was customary for a man to know that one of his main obligations was to intentionally teach the boy in his charge how he could, and why he should, become a man of honor, and that he would have to *earn* that designation through virtuous living. This was true in both pagan and faith-based cultures, the latter based primarily on the Christian tradition. Throughout time, this involved being able to bear increasing responsibilities for him and for others, and eventually becoming worthy of emulation. It was, as C.S. Lewis described, "Men transmitting manhood to men."

In societies as disparate as Sparta, nomadic Africa, medieval Europe, and aboriginal Australia, men mentored boys in their family or clan in those *intentional* and *purposeful* rituals to achieve the designation of "man." Physical, mental, and religious rites of passage involved a boy and his father, or trusted male elders, with one generation guiding the next into adulthood. Fraternal groups from history and mythology helped form the framework and bonds of male camaraderie. Legends grew out of these experiences, becoming part of the culture and the means by which youngsters were inspired and traditions

---

4 Maureen Dowd, *Are Men Necessary?* (Putnam Adult, 2005)
5 Roy Baumeister, *Is There Anything Good About Men?* (Oxford University Press, 2010)

passed down. The absence of training and waning of traditions seem to accelerate the cultural decline, as boys lack any preparation for living virtuously.

In *The Hero with a Thousand Faces*, author Joseph Campbell writes about the hero's journey, one that boys and young men have taken for thousands of years after hearing and answering the "call to adventure," to encounter forces, emerge victorious, return and bestow his knowledge on others. Campbell explored heroic legends of history and myth, such as Jesus Christ, King Arthur, and Sir Galahad in the West, and Rama and Krishna in the East. From them he uncovered common themes of purposeful ritual intentionally leading to a virtuous journey that would lead to heroism.

A hero is best formed during childhood, typically with the help of one who has successfully traveled his own journey. As each understands his heroic purpose and lives it, each fulfills his potential and flourishes, the manifestation of which is demonstrating excellence and virtue, traits that Aristotle considered to be two sides of the same moral coin.

Yet today very little of our culture passes for the ritualized process common to those earlier cultures and their mythologies. Those traditions have been demeaned, devalued and, frequently, discarded. In place of them is nothing that would be recognized by heroes of the past, or by the storytellers who memorialized them.

From my son's early years and onward, I observed chaos in boys and men manifested as the underachieving saggy-pants shuffler, the insecure nice guy, or the bumbling, insignificant fool. Religious faith, a force in virtually every culture throughout time to help know the meaning within and beyond life, has the barest presence in their lives—if at all—thanks to the current expression of moral relativism, as well as to the post-modern philosophy that has permeated our families, schools and houses of worship. These forces have reengineered for the culture at large what it means to be a boy and a man, and what it means to be masculine and feminine. Many bear the responsibility for these changes, under the false mantle of social justice.

Historically, the primary teacher was the father, and he was responsible for modeling what his son must learn. There were others for the boy to emulate as well, be they men in the community or heroes from another age. Societal pillars of school, church, politics and law supported this effort to form the boy's intellect, body, and moral compass, each inspiring him to virtue so that he, too, could do the same good turn. The women in his life supported this by modeling the virtuous and heroic life, instructing, too, by their actions. But over the past half century the culture has turned away from these traditions, causing turbulence that has ripped these pillars from their foundations. The weakened structure bodes an ominous future.

The scourges of divorce and abandonment, with their roots in selfishness, have scattered afar the mentors our boys need, either by choice or courtroom decree. Left behind are confused and troubled youngsters who know little if anything of the tradition of virtue, with mothers who cannot also be fathers. The deterioration of the family, and its associated cultural rites and moral truths, has accelerated since the baby boom generation, thereby causing cynicism, uncertainty, and similar behavior in their offspring. The greatest casualty of this corrosion has been the American boy, because his best model for how to become a man is the father he no longer has around. At this point it is worth emphasizing that girls certainly do suffer as a result of those corrosive changes, as both the social science data and my own experiences confirm that reality; but boys have lost their primary model, and they can therefore no longer identify. While some succeed apart from a heroic parent or mentor, far too many fail on their journey due to parental abandonment or coddling, the latter often to overcompensate out of guilt; and the life that could have been, isn't.

Since parents have ceded their responsibility, government has filled the vacuum by becoming the new father to our children, often in the form of public school. And since the post-modernist philosophy and unearned esteem have permeated the modern American school system, our boys get little that resembles traditional heroic manliness. Of late that seems by design. Indeed, the methodology blurs the genders and sees no need to differentiate the sexes despite how they differentiate themselves—usually to the boys' disadvantage. If a male student behaves in a way that is reflective of his unique brain, he is often perceived as disruptive, and consequently penalized by the politically correct "zero tolerance," "speech codes," or "safe spaces" now in force—or to medication.

While this new "academy" has, unfortunately, become a stronger influence on boys and young men, the opposite has occurred in our religious institutions. The faith-based underpinnings of our culture are corroding, from both our disregard and troubles within. Pew Forum surveys indicate that American Jews are increasingly secular, particularly non-Orthodox Millennials, and consider themselves Jewish by cultural rather than religion.[6] Thus, the modern identity is without its ancient faith. Similarly, Christian churches have a dearth of young and middle-age male congregants. This absence is chosen, to men's discredit, but is encouraged by sexual scandals, politically correct pulpits, and a faith devoid of morality, accountability, or beliefs. Rather than remaining steadfast to the eternal moral truths, church leaders are caving to a culture that increasingly views morality as relative, worships self instead of God, and imagines a Jesus that even *he* wouldn't recognize. Their ranks continue to shrink. These are not the only factors at whose feet we can lay blame.

The sporting life used to be part of the process of helping boys to become men. Its heroes inspired the boyhood passions to achieve—as a good sport. But since many of today's athletes are themselves products of broken homes and poor training, too many of them have little or no knowledge of the traditions noted earlier—and nothing worthwhile to offer their admirers. The self-centered athlete uses sex and drugs as his pillars. But these imposters always crumble, as when he becomes father to children with multiple women but "Dad" to none, or when he fails the drug test, giving lie to the record-setting performance and causing boys to tear up the baseball card or discard the signed football. The latest cause of confusion is the introduction of girls onto boys' teams, in the spirit of new gender—or genderless—*norms*. But since political correctness has now intruded into sports, the truth of the aforementioned is unacceptable—and the decline spreads.

Feminism, in its "First Wave," began as a laudable crusade to insure society's recognition of and honor toward women's equal dignity, and to help gain access to opportunities long denied them. At the same time, however, this "wave" accepted the obvious biological and gender distinction inherent in

---

6 "A Portrait of Jewish Americans" Pew Research Center: Religion and Public life, 10/1/13

the two sexes, and our complementarity. Those efforts have been successful, and we should applaud that success. However, a significant segment, particularly in education, morphed into increasingly militant second and third-wave movements, which seek to deconstruct gender into one whose meaning is "fluid," open to whatever definition each devotee wants, and one whose interest is in enhancing women *at the expense of* men. Should we be concerned about this influence as our boys move from childhood into adulthood? There are several probable outcomes: males and females in constant competition and conflict; males acquiescing due to the penalties from resisting; and, men who enthusiastically conform to this ideology.

The classical heroic theme is important to humanity, because of its focus on elevating the "other" rather than enhancing oneself. But over the past several decades, our leaders in education, media and government have indoctrinated the culture in alternative themes of identity politics and political correctness; and when this is combined with rampant family breakdown and irresponsible men, that virtuous model has never seemed further away—or more important. A culture choosing to discard traditional virtues places itself in jeopardy.

And so this is a rallying cry for those who believe and an appeal to those who do not. Each boy should be given the chance to become, as Galahad did, the perfect knight anointed by God to find his Holy Grail—his noble purpose—and serve others in the same effort. Better still would be to become, as Thomas More had, the perfect example of an imperfect man defending an ancient tradition of moral *truth*. As England's Lord Chancellor under the mercurial King Henry VIII, More humbly abstained from supporting his monarch's decision to divorce his wife and remarry, because she bore him no male heir, and would not acquiesce to his sovereign's demand that More swear allegiance to him as the Supreme Head of the breakaway Church of England. For his adherence to and defense of the truth, he gave up his life—but lives forever in the admiration of many. This part of More's life was dramatized in the play and movie, "A Man for All Seasons."

In Galahad, More, and, hopefully, good fathers, our boys have models to help prepare them to seek their grail and fulfill their purpose, staying true to a well-formed conscience.

Too many boys have been weakened by the new guidelines of society and culture. This dearth of purposeful guidance for excellence and virtue has made boys incapable of beginning their hero's journey, let alone successfully completing it. For morality implies objective standards of right and wrong as well as good and evil, dichotomies abhorrent to the moral relativism of our age. Our salvation hangs in the balance. Boys see heroes, but only in the virtual world of videos. This cultural change leaves boys without the requisite skills and confidence, thereby growing into underachieving adolescents and uninspiring adults.

The consequence of getting this wrong results in too many boys with no hero or mentor, and no desire for the adventure—if they even know of it. So it is parents and their poor decisions that are the primary reason for this trouble, ignorant of the need for ritual or process and thinking that women, schools, and government can teach boys to become men as well as—or better than—male-supervised ritual can.

As I became increasingly aware of these problems, it made me hope that more fathers would become determined to make sure our sons would not live the accidental life; would not meander their way to "wherever" with the modern boy's mantra of "whatever;" and would not confuse themselves during their journeys with their pants low, ear buds in, and hat on backward. Instead of pretending that "it's all good," they need to know that life is often bad but that they can live well in spite of that bad—and then strive to make it right. Boys should at least know what a virtuous man is, and that each could choose to become one—not perfectly imagined, as Galahad was, but imperfectly real, as Thomas More was.

Mankind's great history should not be told without acknowledging bad men; but it cannot be told without noting the importance of virtuous men (and women). I worry that future generations will not have similar stories to tell because their men neglected the virtue tradition—and therefore couldn't write them.

A Boy for All Seasons, but a Man…?

Poor training and poor choices have beaten down the American man, placing the hero's journey—and the promise it offers—in peril for him and his sons. He has lost his way or, worse, departed from it in the belief that this new way is better. But he has it in his power to change, and to choose to become virtuous as the intentional teacher that our boys—and our girls—need. If he meets that challenge, then more heroic men will emerge, helping us to recall the heroes of the past. They will, in turn, inspire future generations of boys to seek the grail and become memorialized, like Galahad was by Tennyson:

> My good blade carves the casques of men,
> My tough lance thrusteth sure,
> My strength is as the strength of ten,
> Because my heart is pure…
>
> Then move the trees, the copses nod,
> Wings flutter, voices hover clear
> "O just and faithful knight of God!
> Ride on! the prize is near!"

CHAPTER 1

The Beginning

*It is part of a good man to do great and noble
deeds, though he risks everything.*

—PLUTARCH

"I NOW PRONOUNCE YOU HUSBAND and wife," confirmed Father George. "You may kiss the bride." At long last! But the final grace that my beloved and I were expecting to share from the sacrament of matrimony had been delayed, as was the kiss for which I so deeply longed, because she couldn't get the ring onto my finger.

For millennia the wedding ring has symbolized a love that is eternal, perfect, and complete. But just as it is with anything sacred, the gift of grace that is perpetually offered to us can only become ours by virtue of our freely accepting it and then living it, thereby fulfilling our purpose. In this case, only by choosing to move my finger into and through the ring's opening could this sacramental love be fulfilled.

As my betrothed continued to struggle with the ring, I became concerned I might not realize this historic divine confirmation of romantic love. We, of course, shared the sanctuary with a man whose hands had been anointed by God, and I thought that only by joining his hands in fervent prayer could we experience what would, perhaps, be only the second wedding miracle in history, thereby allowing my finger to go completely through.

Miracle or not, our determination insured that both finger and ring would each play their respective, preordained parts, so my wife and I could, in turn, play similar roles—as spouses and, ultimately, parents. We knew God had joined us together; therefore, we would let no one tear us apart.

The Hebrew tradition teaches the God-ordained *covenantal* commitment of matrimony of each person to the other, and *their gift of each to the other*. The depth of this commitment is described in Genesis, when God announces his first covenant with Abraham. Using the practice of that time, oath-takers would walk among several animals that had been cut in half, while swearing that if one were to break the covenant then that one would suffer the same consequence as the animals.

The modern secular marriage ceremony has a different emphasis, as it essentially involves a *contractual* agreement involving goods and services *each expects from the other*. Matrimony points to the biblical command that the two become one body; therefore, the well-being of the other is crucial. The fulfillment of this is comparable to Christ being wedded to his church. Since *we* are that church, we are therefore wedded to God. This outward sign, or, more accurately, symbol, is another gift from our Creator. And so Jesus confirms and then completes the original teaching by commanding we should not separate that which God has joined. Anyone who has experienced the trauma of divorce can understand the logic of this, whether or not one is part of any faith.

Our relationship had begun on the romantic love of eros, and then blossomed from the infusion of both the filial love of friendship and agape love from heaven. These are three types of loves that were so elegantly described by the ancient Greeks, based upon definitions far superior to the strictly romantic manner in which we use that word.

Filial love describes a "friendship of equals," and *agape* a "divine" or "charity" love; both evidenced by that which we *do* for the other—by our *actions*—in an act of will and in addition to that which we feel. When one is charitable to another, it is, as Saint Thomas Aquinas said, "to will the good of another." By doing this, we enable the other to know they are loved. Therefore, the depth of this commitment is so much greater than simply the "I love you" sentiment the greeting card industry and Hollywood typically represent. In my marriage there were countless manifestations of this, each fueled by the intimacy and admiration we shared.

The first time my wife and I had a private conversation before our marriage occurred in the hospital cafeteria of our mutual employer; and while I do not remember the topic, I will never forget when she reached across the table and touched my hand. Instantly I felt an electric surge revealing the presence of eros. I tried to hide any effects of this impact, but my occasional loss of concentration during that conversation hinted at my struggle. That touch sparked the greatest romantic love for me, thereby giving proof to its power no matter how slight the brush of a hand when love is the force moving it. I enjoyed that touch for those twenty years because the tenderness and love within her soft and delicate hands made me eager to hold them—and be held by them.

For a marriage to endure it must be based upon that covenantal love. In mine, as with perhaps all, there were periods when only the filial and agape loves seemed present, and my immaturity about how to respond to the seeming absence of eros caused a bit of panic, reminding me of similar feelings that portended the end of earlier relationships. But I eventually realized this was just bad thinking and quite illogical, since my wife was still the same woman who had electrified me. So I decided to focus on the other loves and then use them to regain control over eros, rather than be a passive recipient of the latter's whimsical and fickle nature. I also actively willed my mind to see my wife as I had during our courtship.

It makes sense to think that the willed presence of any of these loves can be like the pilot light, whose flicker can flame by the infusion of the other loves. Of these, charity is the most important; and my wife exemplified that virtue. So that is what we did. We realized the joy of our divine and friendly love, and from that felt the passions return to burn brightly. I loved being a husband. It was work, for sure, but I believed it was the greatest work, equal only to that of being a father. And I loved being able to improve from the steep learning curve and mistakes in the early years.

But more important than having the honor of being *a* husband was the joy of being *her* husband. It was a thrill to know this woman loved me, to know that having my love thrilled her, and to know that neither of us wanted this love to end. My identity had changed because no longer was I just "Thomas," but I was also "Husband." Although I was nowhere near perfect, I still knew it and believed it. I imagined being her Galahad, her knight who would always be there for her, as suggested by this verse written for us by a friend:

> A champion of lost causes, I
> Who reached up to a distant sky
> And found a princess and a knight
> To vanquish gloom and bring the light

Ultimately I became fulfilled in this new relationship, by becoming father to our children: my greatest blessings. She and I were meant to be together, because only through us could Kevin and Maureen have their existence. This marital and family destiny was heralded one day during our courtship, toward the end of an Irish festival on a gorgeous summer day. As the shadows grew long and the crowd thinned, we sat down in the shade to have some ice cream. Looking over her shoulder, I noticed a man walking toward us on the cement path. As he came closer we saw the Roman collar of a priest, and then his smile. Our curiosity grew with his every step.

Upon his arrival we exchanged greetings, and he commented on how lovely we looked together. He was, understandably, especially taken with my date's radiant red hair. We chatted for a few minutes more, and then he offered a blessing that we eagerly accepted. As our new friend began to walk away, he paused, turned his head to look back at us, and softly said, "You are meant to be together, you know." and then smiled with a wink before turning and heading off into the lengthening shadows. Was he our angel? It was a mysterious but welcome surprise. We turned toward each other in a silent but knowing manner that suggested we knew the import of this event. Later that day we, for the first time, revealed our mutual love, and in less than a year we were married.

For most of the next twenty years we knew nothing but that love, as did our children. But as we entered our 21st year her love was gradually withdrawn, an alarming change that portended her eventual departure and the dissolution of our marriage. The experience was, at times, difficult in the extreme; but I gradually became aware that God's purpose for us was also being revealed, and that awareness proved to be a great source of consolation.

As children navigate their way through this challenge and others, they need someone to teach them that those experiences define neither them nor their lives, but instead present them with the prospect of finding greater meaning in those experiences as well as finding greater knowledge of themselves and their abilities to go through these experiences and emerge as better versions of themselves. My hope is that all children become formed in relationships based upon faith, devotion and love, and my prayer is for those children who will not be so fortunate. It is certain that all will travel a journey of some kind; but it is unknown whose will prove heroic.

CHAPTER 2

It's a Boy!

*Before I formed you in the womb I knew you;
before you came to birth I consecrated you.*

—JEREMIAH

Children need models rather than critics

— JOSEPH JOUBERT, FRENCH MORALIST

AS I WATCHED THE NURSES clean my newborn son on the table, I couldn't help thinking, "What a mess." In the modern birth experience, the father is expected to be present, a major change from centuries-old practices in which only women attended to the mother. Oh, for the good old days…

It was with mixed feelings that I participated in this new practice. On the one hand, I wanted to support my wife and be there if something were to go wrong. But on the other hand, I worried this experience would extinguish the flame of romance—one never to burn again. It wasn't pretty; but, as it turned out, I needn't have worried.

While bearing Kevin was certainly a labor of love for his mother, it was also one of pain because of his large head. Its size made the labor long, causing a very, very large nurse to begin throwing her weight around—literally. She took a deep breath, and then while exhaling she flopped her torso fully onto my wife's belly—after which our son soon emerged (so much for high-tech medicine). My wife had done yeoman's work during the pregnancy, dealing with the usual but always-significant discomforts and taking care to eat well. Since we worked in the same hospital, we would regularly enjoy lunches together and then take our "constitutional walk" around the grounds. I marveled at the colorful meals, thinking virtually every nutrient must have been in them—and then in our child.

At Kevin's birth his mother had only a brief opportunity to hold our firstborn, since his large head resulted in her needing some aftercare. I felt badly for my wife, knowing all she had endured during the labor and delivery, let alone during the preceding nine months. This is every mother's heroism, and was certainly hers. And so I held our son as I would a valuable gift, one from God, my wife, and my ancestors, partly because I couldn't know if there would be any more children. The nurses methodically swaddled him in a soft blue blanket and then handed him to me with great care before leaving. Thus it was just father and son in a quiet room with the lights lowered, brought together by a covenantal love—and his big head.

As I cradled him with bear arms, my skin felt soothed by the warmth and softness of his body and blanket. Every once in a while, I would be struck by the value of what lay in my arms, and it filled me with great awe. I'd held kittens, puppies, rabbits, and turtles, but this was remarkably different. When his eyes met mine, I wondered how much he could see. And as we settled in, it seemed that each was exploring the other in the hope of knowing what importance lay behind those portals.

As the emotion of this event wore off and fatigue set in, I eagerly moved us to the large rocking chair nearby and groaned as I sat down. As soon as I had adjusted Kevin into the crook of my left arm, I began the rhythmic motion that would relax the two of us. He would occasionally sigh, and that seemed to loosen my upper back muscles so my shoulders could relax. His eyes were only slightly open, until I softly said, "Hello, Kevin. I'm your father," at which point they seemed to widen as if in recognition of a voice he'd heard for the past nine months, and perhaps an indication of his awareness of the great importance I would be to him. I already knew that in a humble way, and said a prayer of profound thanks, and for the supernatural aid described by Joseph Campbell as the guidance and wisdom of our elders—our guardian angels.

During this tranquil period my imagination moved rapidly forward, and I saw myself carrying my son around on my shoulders, going for walks with his little hand inside mine, and playing all sorts of games together. These activities would seem to be typical of any normal father, knowing he has a loving understudy in whom he can instill his wisdom—gained from past successes *and* failures. That mentoring process should begin at birth, a providential design indicated by Psalm 127: "Behold, children are a heritage from the Lord, the fruit of the womb a reward."

While holding him, I made a commitment to become what God intended and Kevin needed: a better man than I was at the moment and the best father for my son. I wasn't sure what exactly I would do, but knew I would soon figure it out by necessity because we would be together for a while. At that moment, however, I couldn't realize how fast time would pass; but pass it did, I remember thinking on his college graduation day. While watching him process past me adorned in cap and gown to receive his diploma, it seemed that just yesterday his trusting little fingers were reaching for the security of my hand on his first day of school. Instead, my hand would soon feel the grip of one now exuding its own strength and security, reflecting a young man on the way to answering the "call" and declaring further independence during *his* hero's journey. However, Kevin would need to know that no one is ever completely independent, or "self-made," as we all need trusting and loving relationships in order to flourish.

There was much to concern my wife and me about how life would be for our son. News and scholarly reports made me increasingly aware of behavioral and academic troubles that many boys were having, often because of difficulties at home. The most challenging problem was family breakdown, especially divorce. This is particularly harmful for boys, because fathers rarely receive custody of the children. While they may remain in their children's lives, fathers' guidance and influence is usually diminished. It becomes too easy for these men to become physically and emotionally distant, or behave as if they are friends to their children instead of fathers.

The plight of these boys seems destined to continue, judging by data from the 2011 Census Bureau report. It shows that over one-third of American children live apart from their fathers, a threefold increase from 1960. Research repeatedly shows that boys, on average, will disproportionately suffer psychologically, academically, and socially from the trauma of fatherless homes, thereby reducing the likelihood they will flourish. And during this time I also witnessed the diminishing role of faith in the lives of men and boys, and the church pews saw the steady decline of men—and eventually their boys. These changes portended nothing good, as religious faith traditions and the morality they teach have long been a guiding force for humanity.

During the course of writing this book, many college campuses and some big cities have been convulsed by tumult and riots. These disturbances are reminiscent of the turbulent 1960s, as is the current opioid crisis, which is the worst our nation has known. Many in government, education, and local communities attempt to justify or excuse the discord, blaming societal factors such as poverty and drug availability; but they were only partly correct. Unfortunately few, if any, were willing to identify what is arguably the main cause: family breakdown, father absence and the subsequent poverty of *spirit*—a child's discouragement—that those tragedies cause. This cultural chaos seems to reflect family upheaval. Those in the public square wouldn't say that, statistically, upwards of three-fourths of the rioters in some groups had been raised, or were being raised, without a father active in their lives. In that environment a heroic life is extremely unlikely, because the absence of purpose or meaning makes virtue unlikely—if even a possibility.

JOSEPH CAMPBELL'S "HERO'S JOURNEY"

I wanted to increase Kevin's chances for heroism, helping him to find the purpose in his life and then make a mission to fulfill it. This journey, according to Campbell's research, has three phases—Departure, Initiation, and Return—and several aspects to each. Whether the "Call to Adventure" comes from something good or bad, it signals to the boy that an opportunity has opened up for him: to move from the common-day and comfortable known into the risky world of the unknown. Many will decide to refuse the call, thinking the risk is too great; but by avoiding the challenges that could result in honor and virtue, he finds neither. Perhaps he thinks violent or anti-social rebellion is heroic. Or, he only *imagines* himself the hero—and becomes another Walter Mitty. Because of the inherent potential for heroism that life gives us, of many kinds, the life you know is often *not* better than the one you could know—no matter how comfortable you are.

Some, however, answer the call; and whether they do so haltingly or boldly, their step is the first of many that will give them purpose, help them flourish and bring them to fulfillment. In all likelihood, each will need the "Supernatural Aid" of the guidance and wisdom of his elders, described earlier, to prepare for "Crossing the First Threshold," which is the stage during which the boy moves completely away from his comfort zone and fully enters the unknown.

As he moves forward he inevitably must travel "The Road of Trials," face the ensuing tests and then pass them. For they, and his conquest of them, give him what Campbell describes as "momentary glimpses into the wonderful land to help propel him onward." I wanted to share with Kevin some of my past trials, to teach him how well—or how poorly—I had performed during them, and learn from me.

Continuing the Journey

Among these trials, a boy will come upon the "Woman as Temptress," which Campbell defines as any physical pleasure that can challenge a boy's commitment to his journey and ruin him—if he allows it. It is a time when his elders can show him the fleeting nature of this pleasure, and that it is *not* the ultimate joy that awaits him. This can be the most challenging part of the journey for today's boys and young men, because never before has this pleasure been so distracting, so available, and so destructive. This is particularly true for adolescent boys, because in that age group hormonal activity increases dramatically. The "Ultimate Boon" is the time when our journeyman is no longer a boy. He will have achieved excellence with moral formation, attained self-mastery, and become a man. Still, the journey in obtaining the heroic life is not complete.

Heroism is, ultimately, the good that you are *to others*, thereby manifesting its fullness by virtue. It is the unselfish act of freely giving yourself for the benefit of another, an action also known as charity—a love that many mistake as pity. The pride that causes this misunderstanding makes them reject the love that is offered, an action not foreign to many men. Therefore, the only way for a man to become fully heroic is to return from the glory of his achievement and bring his heroism into the regular lives of others. Tragically, the self-centeredness of our culture results in too many men missing this last part.

THE APPRENTICE

In an effort to avoid disaster and fulfill a boy's destiny, a new father should be intentional about forming his son. He should think years ahead about the impact his progeny will have on the world, because it can be for greatness, insignificance, or dishonor. This is the time when the boy's formation will prepare him such that he is willing to leave the comforts of home—particularly the ever-present nurturing of his loving mother—in order to take his journey and successfully complete it. Until birth, the boy's relationship is exclusively with his mother; so only by separating from her can he properly form his masculine identity and, ultimately, his manhood. This is not chauvinism, but a reality seen across cultures and time. This breakaway "may be a difficult and lonely process," notes John A Ashfield, in *Towards an Integrative Perspective on Gender, Masculinity and Manhood*, unless the boy is guided by one who can model the proper way. Mothers absolutely help form a virtuous boy; but the ideal model is Dad, something too many seem to have forgotten.

Until Kevin was approximately five he and I lived in a manner that was reminiscent of the teacher-apprentice experience, because I was home most of the time in preparation to launch a new business, and we spent a great deal of time together. I will always credit my wife for being fully supportive of me and my business formation, and for bearing most of the financial burden for a couple of lean years until it grew. It wasn't easy for us, and especially her; but she showed, once again, heroism in her efforts. It proved to be a great benefit for Kevin and me, early difficulties notwithstanding.

As part of my son's "apprenticeship," I would take him to parks, beaches, and zoos, as well as to town hall, auto shops, and banks. We would visit relatives and friends, or stay home to read, play games, and wrestle. He couldn't have realized it at the time, but the tutelage was underway. I wanted him to experience as much of day-to-day life with me as possible. During rain showers he and I would go for long walks around the neighborhood and explore. He was amazed at the tall trees swaying to and fro from the wind, and the accompanying swooshing sounds. While standing still, he would watch the rain pour off the brim of his hat, smiling with fluttering eyelids at the experience of remaining dry while all around him was wet. That dryness would certainly not last, since every boy knows the reason God made puddles...

Gradually, my son understood more of life, such as a scraped knee not being the end of the world. He learned this because his pain was affirmed but in a controlled manner, and he was unconditionally loved by his parents. He also learned that emotions could be expressed without losing control—most of the time. One day I attempted to treat a rash of his with an antifungal spray, advising him, "This *might* sting a little." Within three seconds the burning sensation broke through all my attempts at reasonableness and the tears poured forth! I felt very bad.

But this was one of his earliest lessons about how a problem can have a good outcome, because when the rash did not sufficiently improve, the doctor's prescription included allowing him to go outside, au naturel, so the fresh air and sun could do what the spray couldn't—but of course only in the privacy of our backyard. After undressing Kevin, I opened the back door, and his wide eyes looked up at me as if to say, "Really, Dad? Can I?" When I said, "Go ahead; doctor's orders!" his big smile grew so large it made me laugh, as did his cry of "Whoopeeeee!" when he bolted out the door. The laughter that ensued—from both of us—was uproarious, as I watched him run around on the grass with a bare derriere. Fortunately, his rash improved in short order, or I might be writing another *Jungle Book*.

Further into his childhood, Kevin and I began a tradition on Saturday afternoons, during which time we would watch an old movie, typically with a heroic theme. Perhaps at least as important was the snack that was always nearby, one that would soon be washed down by a soda. Usually we would sit close to each other with a new bag of potato chips, open it, and then together breathe in the mouth-watering aroma of salt, oil, and potatoes: the staple of our Irish ancestors.

Two particularly significant experiences occurred when Kevin was eleven years old, during and after watching the movies *The Patriot*, and *Gods and Generals*. I always checked the ratings of movies, but for some reason I didn't with *The Patriot*. I just assumed it was a PG-13 movie. But not long into the film, it seemed as though hatchets were finding their way deep into every British soldier, and a great deal of blood and screams were finding their way out. Eventually I paused the film to check the case, and was startled to see the R rating. I considered stopping it; but after taking some time to discuss the movie and how it might help us better understand the events of that tragic war, I was confident Kevin would benefit from watching it and then discussing it further. Similarly, the big-screen depiction of agony and gore in *Gods and Generals* made me take him out of the theater, something that did not please him. As we drove away, I could sense his great disappointment. So I pulled the car over to talk about my concerns, and he expressed his great frustration that I didn't think he was strong enough to handle it—or at least try. The clarity and conviction in his answers suggested a maturity that would allow him to handle the movie or at least try, so we returned to the theater and finished watching it. The discussions that followed both movies, along with the growing confidence I had in Kevin, and which he also sensed, made me conclude it was right to have watched them.

Those experiences reminded me of the only time my very traditional father took some of my siblings and me to a movie. While perusing the local newspaper, he saw an ad for *Don't Make Waves*, starring Tony Curtis and Claudia Cardinale. It was supposedly a comedy about every man's fantasy on a California beach. There is no way my father knew even that much about the movie, or he would never have taken us. I was not quite ten at that time, and two of my siblings were younger. It wasn't long into the film when the steamy romance scenes unfolded. This movie's rating was "approved," and I'm sure that it was by most red-blooded American men. When I recently searched the movie online, I saw its description: "Turn on! Stay loose! Make out!"—words my father certainly never saw while checking the paper, nor ever used. Right about the time steam was shooting out of many ears in that theater, my father stood up and ordered us out of the theater with a quiet but forceful "Let's go." It turned out my father did not see the full title of the movie: "Don't Make Waves, *Make Love.*"

Unlike my experience with Kevin, my father had no intention of having a discussion with me about that movie. He just wasn't that type of guy. Although I sometimes wish he had been, I'm very thankful he was the type of man who respected his wife enough to not watch that kind of movie, and cared enough about his duties as father to raise us according to the morality guided by our faith. He was behaving as a disciplining and perhaps unpopular father, rather than acting as a permissive and more popular "friend." In this experience he was a mentor by his actions more than just words, demonstrating for us how a virtuous man should act. Thinking back, his modeling was reminiscent of the phrase meant for Christian evangelists, urging them to "preach, and if necessary use words." At times I would have preferred words from my father rather than action; but his behavior made more of an impression. The times in my life that I did not act virtuously were the result of me not modeling him enough.

Research on Fathers

For many decades most parental research has been on the importance mothers play in their children's formation, perhaps reflecting the cultural shift that seemed to make males, and the fathers among them, incidental—the distant breadwinner. That was ignorance of history, biology, and logic. Perhaps this thinking was born out of the Industrial Revolution, when many fathers left farms and hometown jobs to work in factories and mines for very long days. This change pulled them away from their sons, but not for selfish reasons. Yet in recent years, there's been an increasing body of research that clearly shows the crucial influence fathers have on the development of their children—for good or bad. And while mothers certainly impart lessons on virtue, as Kevin's mother regularly did, it makes perfect sense that fathers would holistically prepare their sons for a journey to manhood—largely by being able to model it.

Research shows what we should intuitively know, that a married father is more beneficial to his children than one who is involved with them but not married to his mother. "Children," according to Penn State sociologists Juliana M. Sobolewski and Paul R. Amato, "have the highest level of well-being when they are raised in a low-conflict married (i.e., husband and wife) household." Involved fathers have, as noted by W. Jean Yeung, sociologist at the University of Michigan, "a unique impact on children's outcomes." That shouldn't be a surprise; instead, it should be reassuring.

But perhaps the most striking assertion comes from research done by Ronald Rohner, of the University of Connecticut, which shows the great importance fathers are to the health and well-being of their children. He noted in his 2012 report that evaluated more than 500 studies, "We're now finding that not only are fathers influential, sometimes they have more influence on kids' development than moms. Behavior problems and overall adjustment are all more closely linked to a father's rejection of his son than to any rejection by a mother's." He concludes by pointing to results that probably surprised everyone, about the impact on children of their father's love: "Knowing that kids feel loved by their father is a better predictor of young adults' sense of well-being, of happiness, of life satisfaction than knowing about the extent to which they feel loved by their mothers." I hasten to add that Rohner recognizes the importance of mothers, and believes they have been unfairly blamed when children have problems when the onus should have been put on absent fathers. In our case, I knew my wife was very important—necessary—to Kevin and Maureen's formation as *persons*. Her tenderness, nurturing and love were unique to her biology, her gender and, well, *her*. It was only in Kevin's formation into a man, that I was paramount. Thus, the damage to our boys makes a mockery of *no-fault* divorce, and a reason the tradition of marriage is ancient and religion sanctified it.

Life Tests Us

The way each boy meets the challenges along his journey, and the success he has with them, is commensurate with both his age and preparation. A boy facing a tough situation, perhaps from a bully or a tough teacher, could easily lose faith in his father—and in himself—if he finds his dad minimizing the significance of this challenge or too busy to help. That unfortunate response on the part of a father will send the son directly to his mother, so she can nurture the resultant emotional wounds. The father should think back to his own childhood and intentionally see the problem from the same perspective as his son does. And fathers who are inflexible with their sons or who place little value on their feelings risk running afoul of the biblical warning to not provoke their children to anger lest they become discouraged. But neither should dad pity his son.

Kevin's first big test occurred, as it probably does for most children, shortly after he entered first grade. His teacher was well known for being academically excellent, but not for being nurturing or having a mentoring spirit. We would have no concerns about overemphasis on self-esteem. It wasn't long before my son and I found this assessment of her to be accurate. She would have been better suited to older students. For example, she began the year by warning the class about the big troubles they would find if their behavior didn't meet her very high standards, and one punishment would be the public shaming of students by writing the student's name on the blackboard. I do not know if this censure was upsetting to all students, but it was at least somewhat troubling for Kevin. This was a very different experience for him, compared with the nurturing behavior of his two preschool teachers and his parents.

A couple of weeks into the year, Kevin witnessed the first name to be written on the board and the subsequent tears of that student. The event caused a palpable anxiety in him and his classmates. This happened a few more times, and each day he would tell his mother and me about it. Then one night at bedtime, he said to me in a shaky voice, "Dad, I hope I don't get my name on the board." He did not sleep well, and neither did I after he arrived at my bedside to tell me—very early into the morning.

The next morning his pale face and somber demeanor hinted at more anxiety, as did his report of a stomachache. When our neighbor's car pulled into our driveway to take Kevin to school, his anxiety grew, at which point he pleaded with me to take him to school so he didn't have to be embarrassed by being upset in their car. This behavior was a first for him. My son and I paused at the front door; our eyes were locked as we silently pondered *my* next move. Our years together helped build a trusting relationship, so I wanted him to know he could count on me. And I believed this experience was—certainly to him—his time of need. So I told him I would take him, and he responded with a big hug. But my wife and I knew this wouldn't be the end of it, because his bogeyman had to be brought down to size.

On our way to school, I played some soft classical music, hoping to restore a semblance of calm in him. I also gave him a mint in the hope of settling his stomach. A peace seemed to ensue, albeit a tenuous one; but as we got closer Kevin suddenly blurted out with great alarm, "Dad, we're not allowed to have anything in our mouth while at school!" Our proximity to the school was such that I told him to chew the mint and swallow it—much to our mutual regret. It was an Altoid mint, and they are quite strong. All of a sudden I heard him yell, "Dad, I think I'm gonna throw up!" at which point I yanked off my cap and, quickly as I could, reached back to give it to him just in time to catch both breakfast and mint. At that point, hearing Metallica emanating from the speakers instead of Vivaldi would have matched the chaos in the car. But thinking only that his father had heroically sacrificed his hat, not that this very same father had contributed to the problem, he said through his tears, "You're the best dad ever." My bad feelings of guilt were somewhat absolved by those words; words I hoped he would forever want to say.

The solution to his problem, and I imagine with most boys, was not to have him removed from that classroom and put into another; nor was it to have him undergo treatment by counseling or medication. Those actions would have been disastrous because they would have taught him and reinforced in him that he was either inadequate or ill, and needed accommodation for a presumed disability. It would have taught him that he didn't have the resources needed to handle this problem, and perhaps other problems, both in and out of school. And it would have told him that his most important mentor did not believe he could handle it, when in fact I did. Unnecessary surrender is a very bad lesson to teach your child, and especially a father to his son because of how male weakness is viewed in most cultures.

What Kevin needed was more training in how to deal with this next challenge in his life. By doing so we would be developing a template that would become part of his psyche, one he could then apply to the more significant challenges he would face. So with the encouragement of my wife, he and I developed a system in which every night he and I would open our homemade "homework pad," and together we would review and discuss—in detail—his day at school, particularly anything that concerned him. Additionally, I would draw some funny, but not disrespectful, images of his teacher on the pad in an effort to bring her down to size from the monster Kevin had created in his mind. We worked to help his brain associate some humor with his class and good things with school.

Mostly, however, I encouraged him. That is, by reminding him of his strengths, prior successes, and how the virtue of courage is formed when one does the right thing despite how one feels. It wasn't long before my son found the courage within, and began to see himself on the other side of the problem as being in the classroom and learning—with less and less fear of getting into trouble. Or, if he were to get into trouble and get his name on the board, he wouldn't collapse, suffer ridicule or die. Instead, it would give him an opportunity to learn how to recover from a trial. He effectively implemented our plan and successfully finished first grade with that teacher. I still have notes from those sessions, some twenty years later. Oh, and he did get his name written on the board, an experience that he could share with you if you asked him—because he survived!

The Normal Heroism of Fatherhood
I've described only one of several big trials during the early stages of Kevin's journey, and the value of a close relationship between a father and a son. That relationship made it possible for me to give the *aid* to my son, help described

by Campbell as being so important to the traveler on his journey. This is the same relationship I had—and still have—with Maureen. Both Kevin and Maureen had complete trust in me, as I grew to have in them (and which both had with their mother). I'm certainly not inferring I was unusually heroic during those experiences, as I believe any normal father would demonstrate that behavior. And my wife was always supportive of my efforts, and gave her own as well. The heroism that perhaps I showed was being there in Kevin's times of need and giving of myself in order to advise and guide him. That is what fatherhood should be, but what it increasingly is not. More importantly, I had been there to help form him during the normal times leading up to those occasions.

Those templates I mentioned earlier are embedded into Kevin's mind and heart; They are the result of guidance and modeling he received from me, which he would be able to apply when facing other tests along his journey—and when others need his guidance, his virtue and his heroism. Only by giving that help will he become heroic. And in order to be in that position to help, he must demonstrate his abilities and self-control as he moves gradually away from his father and into the competitive world of his peers.

CHAPTER 3

Peer Review

This late dissension grown betwixt the peers...
History of Henry VI Act III Scene I

—WILLIAM SHAKESPEARE

ARISTOTLE DESCRIBED HAPPINESS AS "AN activity of the soul in accordance with virtue" and our striving for this as being "the highest good." In this striving, a boy must learn to moderate himself and avoid extremes or excesses of any kind—particularly in his interactions with people and the associated circumstances. This is Aristotle's "Golden Mean," or equilibrium. Without this ability, a boy would risk the flitting to and fro that seem common to so many boys today, behavior that is exemplified in Robert W. Service's rhythmic line in "The Men That Don't Fit In":

> So they chop and change, and each fresh move
> Is only a fresh mistake.

Those men described by Service seem to be failed "misfits," a destiny, increasingly, of too many boys these days. However, awareness of the confused state of our culture, politics and schools made me encourage Kevin and Maureen to avoid wanting to "fit in" to that confusion. During the school-age years that lead up to adolescence, a boy's interactions with peers will allow for continuous self-evaluations. The greatest lessons often result from disagreements, especially those that force him to either flee or fight. If it is the latter, in a justifiable defense, then the challenge is to be aggressive without the extreme of uncontrolled violence.

Boyhood Conflict

My initial experience with this as a parent occurred while our family attended a family barbecue, after my children had made their way from the porch into the backyard to join approximately a dozen children who were playing games. I began to watch them play, and was, as usual, thoroughly enjoying the lively activity and competition that children always bring to gatherings. Both sexes had voluntarily segregated themselves by their "binary, cisnormative" gender roles, as has occurred throughout human history. This was no surprise, because the non-binary, gender-fluid activists had yet to emerge in our culture. The girls seemed to be cooperating amongst themselves quite nicely, while the boys quickly manifested their competitive spirit with each other.

From my vantage point on the screened-in porch, I watched as the events unfolded. It was easy to spot my three-year-old daughter, Maureen, near the swing set at one side of the yard because of her blond hair, colorful clothes, and dancing—the latter stemming, as usual, from an ever-present song in her head. She was happy with the swirling activity of children and dogs, so I knew she was OK. But how was my son faring? When I turned to find Kevin, seven years old at the time, my attention was captivated when he suddenly became involved in a pushing competition with the group of boys his age, partly because a shove can escalate in a flash.

It wasn't until I began writing this book that I remembered how differently I reacted to each of my children. Upon seeing Maureen, I was exclusively an observer, however enthusiastic. I am certain I would have seen some of myself in her if, say, I found her behavior wanting. But with Kevin, I immediately saw myself in him with everything he was doing, as in my mind he was a smaller, younger version of me. It was also due to my having had my own share of childhood shoving and wrestling matches, and knowing how stressful these challenging crucibles are that boys traditionally face as rites of passage. And these point to the identification that one male has with another.

The psychoanalyst Erik Erikson reportedly said that shortly after boys become aware they have behinds, they become infinitely interested in who can kick whose. That statement seemed to be borne out on this day, when one husky boy began to get a little too pushy with the others and then turned his attention toward my son. They could easily be caricatures of good and evil, since the scowling instigator had course, jet-black hair while Kevin, the defender, had golden locks and an even demeanor. He was not the type who would start a fight, so I was interested in how he would handle this.

The boy took two menacing steps toward Kevin and pushed him, causing me to tense a bit. So much rides on a boy's response to his first pugilistic challenge. To my pleasure, Kevin gave it right back. That commenced the shoving contest, at which point the laws of nature seemed to take over. Each boy went back and forth with their respective shoves, and as their movements accelerated and the intensity increased, the circle of onlookers grew. This circle widened to give the combatants more room—and to lessen the risk of its members becoming a casualty of the activity. I briefly turned to my right in order to check on Maureen. She had frozen in her tracks, her blue eyes blazing intently at the sight of her brother's first "fight." God help those who would hurt her "Kevvy."

The two boys moved around with arms flexed, hands opened, as each sized up his combatant. Their brains rapidly assessed information obtained from the first few shoves in preparation for the next one. They then charged each other as if they were bighorn rams ready to butt heads. Recalling the damage Kevin's big head had caused his mother, I wondered if any observers watching this encounter would immediately cry "Foul!" It was the other boy's good fortune that there wasn't a direct hit.

After the grunts of the collision, they separated, each circling the other like the animals they seemed to be. With cheeks reddened, hair mussed, and shirttails whipping around in the scuffle, they again went at it, causing some parents to rush toward them to restore the peace. But before they could get there, Kevin had maneuvered his opponent sufficiently to put him off balance, thereby allowing the laws of physics and gravity to "assist" that boy to the ground.

While glad for the outcome, I was proud of Kevin's willingness to stand his ground in order to handle his first combative experience. But what if he had not prevailed in that backyard bout? Would that have been a failure? In one sense it would. Yet his willingness to mix it up, defend himself, and be engaged in this "arena" would still have made *him* a success despite the failure of his *effort*. He had not started this contest, but had stayed in it. I, of course, couldn't have known it at the time, but this experience was a harbinger of future contests of a similar nature, because Kevin ended up wrestling throughout high school. And I would become as proud of him during those contests as I was during this backyard event—whether or not his arm was raised in victory.

Upon arriving home, I made sure to talk with Kevin about the dustup, because this was a great teachable moment. He needed both my affirmation and approval of his actions to know he was just in defending himself, and that I would have had his back if another parent had gotten involved. I also wanted him to know that I believe most disagreements should be resolved using one's intellect and reasoning skills, but that anger and aggression are sometimes required in the defense of that which is right. Again we turn to Mr. Service in his poem "Carry On":

> It's easy to fight when everything's right,
> And you're mad with the thrill and the glory.

This was Kevin's first "just war"—his righteous self-defense and restoration of order.

Humans are not born with virtue, but Saint Augustine, the great African bishop, as if echoing Aristotle, asserted its development if it "succeeds to them as the result of learning," and then doing. "Practice makes virtue" are words one could reasonably attribute to both Augustine and Aristotle. Interaction with others along a boy's journey, however fraught with risk, facilitates that education. And who better to teach the boy than his father—provided he has any virtue to impart to his son.

A couple of years later, Kevin would make me recall this important concept while he and Maureen were playing in the snow with an older neighborhood boy in our front yard. I happened to be upstairs walking by a window and looked down just in time to see this boy drop a huge block of snow on Maureen's little head. In a flash, that boy was on his back, the result of a brother's righteous defense of his sister's honor. He helped Maureen get up and wipe off the snow, after which the offender was sent packing.

These stories are examples of the inevitable tests a boy must face while growing up. Far better for the boy who receives mentoring along this road and receives the encouragement described by Service:

Carry on! Carry on!
Fight the good fight and true;
Believe in your mission, greet life with a cheer;
There's a big work to do, and that's why you're here.
Carry on! Carry on!
Let the world be the better for you;
And at last when you die, let this be your cry:
Carry on, my soul! Carry on!

CHAPTER 4

Declaration of Independence

To find yourself, think for yourself.

—Socrates

During my childhood in South Orange, New Jersey, a town next to Newark, I never walked uphill to and from school in knee-deep snow, but I did walk to and from kindergarten, at a school several blocks away. However, once first grade started, I had to ride the #31 public transit bus home from school to a stop on a very busy avenue that was also several blocks from my home.

We were instructed to keep away from strangers, and I did. During one walk home from the same bus stop during my seventh grade year, I became aware in my periphery that a car going in the same direction had slowed. This slow pace was made all the more noticeable because the street was a busy thoroughfare. The man driving the car called out and offered me a ride home. I was old enough to know the "home" to which he referred was not going to be mine, and therefore ran through several backyard shortcuts in order to get to my house. As I related this to my father, I could see the skin around his jaw tighten as his muscles flexed. He immediately stood while putting out his cigarette, and then walked determinedly outside toward the street. He stared down one side of the street and then the other, but nothing came of it.

At the time, being out on one's own was commonplace for most children, but after having children of my own, I learned how different things are for today's children. Safety and adult-organized activities are greatly emphasized, but this sacrifices the independence of too many children. In contrast with my childhood experiences, I was troubled by the new state of affairs facing my children.

The Stranger Danger Obsession...and Letting Go

One of Kevin's early actions, suggesting he was now open to his hero's journey, proved to also be a test for me. It occurred one Sunday in early spring while driving home from church, after we had stopped in town to get some doughnuts. He was six or seven years old at the time, and on our way out of the store he said he wanted to walk home by himself. The distance was several blocks, and was a big deal for him, but it shouldn't have been for me. After thoughts about safety shot across my mind, I let Kevin go, but as he walked up the street, I briefly shadowed him in our car. When suddenly he turned and spotted our car I saw the frown on his face—a frown I am sure was directed mostly at me—making me feel embarrassed as I drove away. It bothered me that he turned to check, because that meant he didn't trust me to let him go. He was right.

Not long after getting home, I thought about this and realized I was becoming influenced by the modern, fear-driven life, one engineered by constant warnings from the media, schools, police, and neighbors about danger presumably lurking around every corner. Headlines screamed "Stranger Danger!", "Razor-embedded Apples!", "Toxic Tap Water!"—events that are rare, if not imagined. Society had changed the norms about how to raise children, somehow thinking it knows better than parents. And if you go against those norms, you risk a harsh penalty.

It struck me that Kevin was being held back from answering the call to adventure by both the local culture and his parents. But I take most of the responsibility for that because mothers, designed as they are for nurturing, tend toward overprotectiveness. I had let the alarmists affect me, and was therefore not allowing my son the freedom he needed—and very much wanted. So I changed, although not as fast as he and I wanted, because our immediate sphere mostly contained very cautious parents, making it difficult to find others who were thinking in the same manner. A playdate was sometimes OK for them, but rarely if ever was it OK for most children to just open the door and go off to play.

So Kevin began to explore the woods surrounding our neighborhood. He then rode his bike into town with the freedom to navigate the intertwining streets from a different perspective, one that did not involve bicycling with his father or looking through our car window. In time he would demonstrate just how great his desire was to explore, by traveling and working throughout the world via all sorts of conveyances, including his feet, and experiencing many more neighborhoods. He returned not long ago, only to leave again via a more powerful two-wheeler on his way to exploring the Americas.

Answering the Hero's Call

There are many journeys a boy can take, but not all will show him to be heroic because, being imperfect, he will not always demonstrate virtue. Many are unaware a hero's journey even exists, and are therefore ignorant of its beckoning call. On whichever journey they make, many will get lost along the way—particularly from adolescence onward. Or, some will refuse the responsibilities, and therefore choose to either ignore the call or quit early on. But they do so at their own peril, risking a life unfulfilled and marked by regret. Joseph Campbell described the challenge this way: "The cave you fear to enter holds the treasure you seek." In *Moby Dick*, Herman Melville describes the turbulence of the sea and the tranquility of land, and then compares this contrast with that which lies within us: "For as this appalling ocean surrounds the verdant land, so in the soul of man lies one insular Tahiti, full of peace and joy." He then concludes with a description of a life referring to those who chose *not* to answer the call, or who did so absent virtues such as courage or fortitude: "But encompassed by all the horrors of the half-lived life."

The legends and mythologies explored by Campbell seem to indicate that most of the journey must occur in the unknown and unexplored reality. And even if we gradually become familiar with the "cave" he describes, we still know neither the outcome nor how we will act. By meeting the challenges leading up to adolescence, planned or spontaneous, a boy grows in character, competence, and confidence. As he successfully works his way deeper into the journey, he approaches a manhood that has been years in formation, ultimately gaining that title after giving witness of his virtue by his service to others.

It is natural to be wary, if not fearful, about the unknown, but a mentor can encourage a boy during his exploration. Deprived of this guidance, he will most likely remain bound rather than free like the almost-hero in Tagore's ironically titled poem "Hero," who can only imagine his heroic deed:

> A thousand useless things happen day after day, and why
> Couldn't such a thing come true by chance?
> It would be like a story in a book.

For too many boys, the heroic potential remains in the book.

CHAPTER 5

Multi-Cultural Manhood

He that breaks a thing to find out what it is has left the path of wisdom.

—Gandalf, *The Fellowship of the Ring*

In all likelihood, the challenges of today's boys would be unrecognizable to most, if not all, earlier cultures. Throughout most of America's past and indeed the world's, there was an expectation that a boy would move from the potential within the "being" of his birth to the "becoming" and then "arriving" of his manhood—a transformation that would be celebrated for its own sake as well as for the sake of the community.

These traditions formed because men knew the importance of helping boys mature, so they would be ready to take the lead when those men had passed their prime. The process inspired both the mythological and historical legends, and each inspired the other. Ancient and cross-cultural records indicate the presence of traditions to be followed before a boy attained manhood, and several themes are common in all of them. The men of a family or village typically trained boys in the ways of man and nature, to provide food, shelter and protection for themselves and for others, and made requirements of them to demonstrate their mastery of these lessons.

Manhood Around the World

The stages of the hero's journey are essentially the same for mythic men, such as Hercules, Achilles and Odysseus, or those in history from throughout the world, such as those of the Masai or Luhya tribes. Both African groups require boys to engage in a long and intensive training regimen, one consisting of multiple levels of difficulties and responsibilities led by seasoned warriors, spiritual leaders and tribal elders, in an effort to develop skills that would make them the future providers and protectors of the tribes. The Masai training traditionally culminated in a successful solo hunt of a male lion. The male elders in the Luhya tribe regularly counseled their boys about what was expected of their growth into manhood and how to achieve it, eventually teaching them to live independently of the tribe and then interdependently with each other. This teaching would, for example, help them learn to build huts in which each would live and to provide the necessary training that would allow the group to live well. Camaraderie was important for both groups, as it provided the encouragement that proved helpful to them as they strove to complete the arduous challenge. When they finally returned home, the village celebrated their arrival because they had returned as men to the benefit of the tribes.

The family or tribe prepared boys in the Viking culture for manhood, raising them in a way completely foreign to today's parents. A boy typically spent the first five years of his life with his family, having intensive tutelage by his father and brothers. After that, he was sent to either an elder male relative or a trusted male community leader to receive rigorous training to become skilled in many areas vital to their social order. These included farming, animal husbandry, construction, and seamanship. He was also required to become a highly skilled warrior, using both hand-to-hand techniques and weaponry. Remarkably, by the time a Viking boy reached the age of ten, he was considered to be a man. The skills weren't learned in isolation, but in the context of how important they were to the thriving and continuation of their social order.

These societies demonstrated the importance of their boys successfully completing the systematic process of earning manhood, in part by publicly celebrating their achievement. This celebration implied, and therefore helped instill, confidence, as it expected the departing boys would return as young men. Take note: failure was *not* esteemed, and certainly not celebrated; but lessons were learned from it.

Our early Indian tribes are commonly thought of as warriors, but this would be an incomplete understanding. The Sioux Nation tribes, for example, believed that each boy had the potential for developing a specific talent in order to benefit the tribe, such as woodcraft, hunting, or artisanship, and as the boy matured and became skillful at the trade, he could eventually teach the next generation of boys and perpetuate the traditions.

Today one needn't replicate the life-threatening challenges of some of these rituals, and the much longer life expectancy is due, in part, to advancements in science and technology, and a reason why we don't need to force manhood on our prepubescent males as the Norse culture did. But as we advanced, we discarded the good aspects of the aforementioned cultures, mainly the traditions of *purposefully and intentionally defining and teaching manhood*—one based upon achievement and virtue, and then the celebration to honor it. However, in too many of today's homes, *if* a celebration does occur, it is often independent of a measurable success—and often minus a father. Today, the closest most American males can come to having the Masai experience is to vacation in Kenya and participate in a simulated Masai warrior training camp—where no lions are hunted!

Intellectual Manhood

While some cultures of medieval Europe conferred manhood based more upon physical prowess and gallantry, as the knight's code of chivalry indicated, others saw intellectual prowess as the measure of a man because it indicated mental ability and the consequent control over oneself as well as others. In *From Boys to Men: Formations of Masculinity in Late Medieval Europe*, Ruth Mazo Karras describes a parallel track to manhood: "Like knights, students could compete in combat, but through intellectual disputations," thereby making cerebral performance the measure of the scholar's manhood.

Similarly, the Jewish tradition prepared its boys for the designation of "manhood" through a rite of passage involving scholarship. Contrasting the Jewish concept of manhood with, say, the warrior model, David Gilmore, in *Manhood in the Making*, notes "Their avenue of success has always been intellectual, to live by one's wits." Successful completion of the Bar Mitzvah and the eventual challenges of being a dependable man and good provider would earn a Jewish man the honorific "Mensch." Unlike the earlier cross-cultural practices noted above, in which manhood was designated and celebrated only *after* a lengthy process, today's surveys indicate there is much more preparation for the post-ceremony party than there is on the boy's attainment of true spiritual manhood in line with Abraham, Isaac and Jacob.

Worldwide, cultures have long required boys and adult males to perform and achieve in order to develop their masculinity and fulfill their manhood. The designation was determined by what you could do, how well you did it, and how often you used your skills for others. And it all makes sense considering, from the beginning, how men have *always* been the builders, providers and protectors.

Vanishing Fraternal Organizations
YMCA

In 1844, 22-year-old George Williams, a devout Christian from Great Britain, had become increasingly concerned about the troubles rural young men faced in decadent London, after they had moved there to find work. So he led a group of them in founding the Young Men's Christian Association as a sanctuary whose main purpose was the "improvement of the spiritual condition of young men engaged in houses of business." But if George Williams were alive today, I doubt he would recognize his YMCA.

By World War II, women and families had been allowed partial entry because the men were at war, women were needed in factories to support the war effort, and daycare was needed for their children. Gradually, women were permitted to take on a greater role, and there was no going back to the YMCA's roots of being a fraternal organization for men.

In 2010, the organizational logo of the YMCA was changed to "The Y," and according to a *female* executive, one reason was "…so that it is immediately apparent that everything we do is designed to *nurture* (emphasis added) that potential of children and teens." Besides noting the obvious demotion of "M" and "C" from the logo, I wondered if there were no qualified men to fill this key position. I was also struck by the new mission of this organization, which is "to nurture," a natural and traditional attribute of females, and not, say, "to build," an historic activity hard-wired into males. Upon opening the "Y" website at the time of this writing, I was struck by the number of photos representing women and girls, an oddity (at best) for a traditionally fraternal organization. A random search of various sections for the word "men" and then "women" resulted in 66 and 67 references, respectively. And the organization's principle is described this way: "At the Y, strengthening *community* (not "boys" or "men") is our cause."

YWCA

It was more than 150 years ago that the Y**W**CA was formed, for reasons similar to the founding of its male counterpart, and it has grown to be all about empowering women. How striking it was to learn that "Women" and "Christian" are still part of the organization, in contrast to the trimmed "Y." It seems, in its efforts to empower women, it relies greatly, if not exclusively, on its own sex. A check of their website at the time of this writing revealed an organizational profile that showed *no* male names, and while there were some references to men, there were far more references to women. Whether or not one agrees with its current motto, "Eliminating racism, empowering women," one can admire the YWCA for its boldness in stating the desire to inspire *its* sex. Would that we could have seen that same boldness for male focus and empowerment on the YMCA site—and elsewhere in the Y**M**CA.

CYO

At its inception in the 1930s, the Catholic Youth Organization's emphasis was on building the character of Catholic boys through a program of athletics, moral development and justice, with the aim of forming virtuous men. Its founder, Bishop Bernard J Sheil of Chicago, saw the results of boys falling off the straight and narrow during his prison ministry, and sought to positively influence them in their formative years through mentoring, hoping to keep them productive members of society. Initially, boxing was the only sport, and girls were not involved. Not long after the CYO was formed, it began admitting girls, and it has since grown into a comprehensive *co-ed* program of faith building, using sports as a vehicle.

Boy Scouts

In 1908, Englishman Robert Baden-Powell, a wartime hero and proven leader of men, began an organization aimed at doing for boys what he had done with the men under his leadership: teaching skills to survive and thrive in one's life, and to do so in a moral and honorable way. With that aim, the Boy Scouts was formed. And from their manual we see their oath, their motto and a great explanation of both:

"On my honor I will do my best to do my duty to God and my country, and to obey the scout law; to help other people at all times; to keep myself physically strong and mentally awake and morally straight."

Their motto brought fame to two simple words: *Be Prepared*. "Be prepared for what?" someone once asked Baden-Powell. "Why, for any old thing," he replied, and then continued: "The training you receive in your troop will help you live up to the Scout motto." But Baden-Powell could not have imagined that his organization field manual would need revision to help prepare his charges to one day accept—by implicit or explicit force—an eight-year-old girl identifying as a boy. Were he still alive and in charge, his history suggests he would be sympathetic to this troubled youngster, but his morality would assert the truth of her reality while dismissing the pretense of this fantasy—especially in one so young and so far from maturation. And Baden-Powell would have had both natural sense *and* science behind his assertion, since just three years earlier American scientist Nettie Stevens had published her discovery of the xx/xy female/male (i.e., girl/boy) chromosomal distinction! One wonders, but not for long, what reaction he would have to a *cub* scout coming in one day, and asserting that he—or she—had decided to identify as an *Eagle* Scout...

The YMCA, CYO and Boy Scouts are cited in order to show examples of programs that, while doing good work, were once part of society's structures designed solely for the purpose of forming boys into faithful and virtuous masculinity and manhood. They formed friendships, camaraderie and moral support through the *identification* of one man with another, and great mentoring traditions of initiation and achievements were born—but which are no more. Our society has become transient, fractured and isolated, such that too many boys and men don't have the relationships held so dearly in prior generations, and so necessary to a full life. That is one reason for the popularity of the sports entertainment industry, a use of time that has little beneficial consequence because it is passively watched. And the recent infiltration of women and a progressive political agenda into this industry has affected its popularity with men. The change in fraternal relationships will continue to have cultural repercussions, but never more than the absent relationship between a boy and his father.

Intentional and Purposeful Neglect

The "bliss," or deep spiritual joy, described by Campbell of the journey with a virtuous purpose would seem to be welcome by all boys—but how will they learn about it? Today's new approach uses television shows and commercials as the classrooms, relying on "half-men," "beer-men," and "wo-men" to be the teachers, since virtuous men seem to be absent. The music industry provides much of the lesson plan for language arts; and this plan does not include English as it has long been known, but rather a deformed and stunted version of the language that uses vulgarity to incite boys to aim low, disrespect women, and glorify anarchy as well as themselves. Each day popular music entertainers—of *both* sexes—disrespect and degrade women by their lyrics, clothing and general behavior; so by doing this, they make their marches, hashtags and protests ring hollow. Sadly, many girls have chosen to admire them.

In a 2003 study of adolescent and middle-aged Australian males, published in the Electronic Journal of Sociology, researcher David Crawford, of the University of Western Sydney, found that no member of his research group could define "being a man" nor identify when he believed he had become one. This is not surprising, since the survey also revealed that none had given any thought to "becoming a man," making me believe this subject was not taught to them as children—particularly by their fathers. His conclusion has what should be interpreted as a sobering alert, "Masculine development is presently left to chance in Australia and other Western Cultures." That is the exact *opposite* of having an intentional and purposeful plan.

Bat-Manhood

Were Kevin to ask me when it was that I thought I could be labeled a "man," I might describe the times, for example, when I had defended my sister Carolyn against some misbehaving guys. But it might be more accurate to describe the variety of experiences I believe contributed to the process of me becoming the man I am today, including those in which I had failed to measure up but from which I ultimately learned. Contrary to David Crawford's research subjects, over time I became increasingly aware of the concept of the "manhood" I sought to achieve, and how that would change as I matured. Certain men influenced that maturation; particularly those who I believed exemplified that title. My father comes to mind.

I cannot ever recall a time when I doubted my Joseph Caffrey's manhood; but it wasn't until after he passed away shortly before I turned thirty, that I felt humbled by aspects in which he towered over me. For example, I can recall many a Sunday afternoon during my childhood, when my father would drink a tonic to ease his upset stomach. I was too young to know why, but later learned that the cause was a miserable boss under which he worked for nearly a decade. I'm sure my father dreamed often of telling his boss where to go, and then imagined the work he would much rather do; but bursting that bubble was the realization that he had ten bodies to feed, shelter and clothe, and off to work he would go. That's heroism. That's manhood. Would it rub off on me?

My father and I shared an experience late one night during my thirteenth year, when a bat had flown into our old Victorian house while my four sisters and I were watching *The Saint* on TV. This event sent my shrieking siblings diving under cushions and tables, each in a desperate attempt to avoid the dreaded "bat-in-the-hair" horror. Christine, Linda and Carolyn were able to get partially underneath the cushions of their respective chairs, leaving little Claire to squeeze underneath the coffee table.

In response, I ran upstairs to tell my father, who, to my chagrin, simply said, "Take care of it." His response may have been motivated by a strong desire to go back to sleep, after having endured another rough day at the office, but I prefer to think that it stemmed from a desire to move his fourth son that much closer to manhood. So I grabbed a towel from the linen closet, folded it in half and then descended the stairway three steps at a time before landing in the foyer at the peak of the screams. Had a Hollywood producer of horror movies been within a mile of our house, he would have quickly found his way to it in order to sign each of my sisters to a contract. I opened the large front door and tried to encourage the bat to exit, but it persisted in its chaotic loop through the living room, dining room and foyer. Each time it came upon me I swung in a huge adrenalin surge, but missed. It made me wish I had spent more time in our backyard, trying to hit the knuckleball pitches thrown by my brother Paul.

As my sisters' nemesis neared me once more, I took a deep breath, readied the towel, and then took a forceful swing while grunting loudly in the process—to finally make contact! The animal slammed into the stairway, at which point I leapt to place the towel over the little beast and then pounded the remaining life out of it.

Returning to the imagined question asked by my son at the beginning of this story, I could easily respond with tales such as my "bat-man" experience and others noble—or not so—each of which helped move me away from boyhood and toward manhood, and which contributed to the yardstick for that measurement. Heroism *always* denotes the presence of virtues, because we can only know the existence of courage or temperance while they are being demonstrated. We become heroic only after we have *lived* heroically, and that is an ongoing process. So whenever it is that boys and their mentors think they have arrived at some designation of "manhood," each must remember that that status is always a process of *becoming*. Each day presents opportunities to *become* more of a "man."

SMALL EXPECTATIONS

Having abandoned our traditions, we are a society without a standard against which each young male can measure himself—if he (or we) even cares. Bret Stephenson, author of *From Boys to Men, Spiritual Rites of Passage in an Indulgent Age*, writes, "America now has the longest period of adolescence of any country." In his other professional role, Stephenson is founder and director of "The Adolescent Mind," an enterprise that incorporates into its business model the wisdom and traditional practices of native peoples, all aimed to assist at-risk and high-risk adolescents—particularly boys—to find their virtuous purpose as they move into manhood. As for America's propensity to extend its children's transition into adulthood, Stephenson notes how striking a contrast this is when compared with the practice of many indigenous cultures throughout millennia, each of which aimed to greatly shorten that adolescent period out of necessity, no doubt, but also on principle.

Much should be required of our boys to make heroism possible. The common requirements can and should be demanding, especially with increasing competition against counterparts from around the world. However, if little is expected of our boys, then they will not likely demand much of themselves due to the perceived discomforts or inability to proceed.

The practices described in earlier cultures are in stark contrast to our modern method of educating boys, which involves the imaginary world of virtual technology and the female-oriented school world. Both of these require insufficient use of boys' bodies and brains, and nothing related to masculinity and manhood. They do become experts in safe spaces, trigger warnings and tolerance, and learn to swim in the fluid currents of the gender-identity pool. But both the social science data and the need for industries such as "The Adolescent Mind" indicate that boys need a different expertise.

If asked, most fathers would surely want their sons to grow up to become virtuous men. But the problem is the absence of any intentional plan to do this, and therefore no system to achieve that noble goal. Perhaps fathers are unsure of their own manhood—or at least their virtue. Maybe one day this dynamic will change. If not, then the only hope is that, upon self-reflection, those boys and men will feel the spur of a dissatisfied life and interpret that as Campbell's "Call to Adventure"—and then answer it.

CHAPTER 6

Media *Does* Matter

Everything I learned, I learned from the movies.

--Audrey Hepburn

One evening during the early 1960s, I sat down to watch a television show in the family living room and became transfixed by the opening scene that would soon become iconic. *Crack, crack, crack...crack*! exploded from the speaker, as this unknown man fired twelve hip shots with lightning speed from his trademark Winchester Repeater rifle. Riveted to my seat, I could feel the adrenaline surging as I watched my first episode of *The Rifleman*. Oh, how I loved that program! And in short order, the man handling that rifle became a hero to me as well as to the wild territory of his time.

As I think back about that show, I know it is a striking example of the heroic nature of our media culture—but from a time that has long since passed. It starred Chuck Connors as the widowed homesteader Lucas McCain, and co-starred Johnny Crawford as Mark, his only child. The storyline depicted McCain's efforts to properly raise his son in the rough New Mexico territory of the late 1800s. It was one of many Westerns in the fifties and sixties, and heroic virtue was always the theme.

McCain was a tall, fit man, one who was renowned in the territories for being skilled with his unique weapon—but only in the pursuit of justice. That was the gun's purpose, and McCain was intentional in teaching his son the nobility of that purpose. Some might complain about the violence in the show, but they would be guilty of presentism: interpreting historical events by today's standards. This was the Wild West in the late 19th century, when guns were considered an essential part of a man. And in some of the same parts of our country, they still are.

In his efforts to properly raise his boy, McCain would frequently use another tool, the Bible, and refer to it whenever he was teaching his son about the moral dimension of a particular situation. He was an example of "those divine teachers" described earlier by Pope Pius XI, who extolled them as being virtuous. At the conclusion of each episode, the producers faded out with an image containing both his rifle and Bible. The state of today's culture makes me wonder which of the two it finds more offensive.

It was clear that McCain was also a devoted and loving father, using a great combination of toughness and tenderness with his only child. And these roles weren't difficult for either of the actors. At Connors' death, Crawford said of his on-screen dad, "He was always interested in me and ready to offer advice…and help. It was a good experience for me to spend time with Chuck and learn how he dealt with people. I learned a great deal from him. He was just my hero."

So Lucas McCain certainly was an example of a man's man. But he was also a woman's man, as his respect for that sex was always evident by his manners and protective efforts. In every episode he demonstrated all of the cardinal virtues, and he is an example of what boys could become and what women could love. He was reminiscent of Galahad.

The other media hero of my childhood was *The Lone Ranger*. Each episode began with the staccato blare of a lone trumpet, urging on the "masked man" in his hot pursuit of the enemy. This heat came in the form of his trusty white steed, Silver, who exploded into a full gallop upon hearing his master's cry, "Hi-Yo Silver, away!" And just like Lucas McCain, the Ranger demonstrated the virtue of courage by always running *toward* trouble rather than away from it, striving to serve others in great need. To this day, no piece of music thrills me more than the soaring finale of Rossini's "William Tell Overture," which became the theme music of the show. In fact Kevin and, especially, Maureen, would ride their rocking horse with great fervor each time I played that dramatic piece.

Underpinning the Ranger's actions was a moral code, one that encourages personal integrity and responsibility while asserting certain absolutes. The following statement of beliefs must seem quaint to some, and anachronistic to the post-modernists of today, but to many—including me—they are eternal certainties:

"I believe...

- That to have a friend, a man must be one.
- That all men are created equal and that everyone has within him the power to make this a better world.
- That God put the firewood there, but that every man must gather and light it himself.
- In being prepared physically, mentally, and morally to fight when necessary for what is right.
- That a man should make the most of what equipment he has.
- That this government of the people, by the people, and for the people shall live always.
- That men should live by the rule of what is best for the greatest number.
- That sooner or later...somewhere...somehow...we must settle with the world and make payment for what we have taken.
- That all things change but truth, and that truth alone, lives on forever.
- In my Creator, my country, my fellow man."

I loved both characters, but never could I have imagined that one day I would identify with Lucas McCain in what would prove to be my destined role as a single father.

Toward the end of the 1960s, the counter-cultural tumult had affected the media industry. As time went on, we increasingly saw sarcasm, cynicism and irony in male characters. Intelligent masculinity seemed to be on the wane.

A Boy for All Seasons, but a Man...?

Over recent decades, the media industry has presented us with men unsure of their identity and their place at work and at home. Or we see masculinity redefined from that which we have known since the beginning. Males are too often portrayed (many willingly) as bumbling fools, uncouth slobs, or as being generally unsure about themselves. And if portraying a male religious figure, the character will almost certainly be without virtue. One is far more likely to see a scandalous priest or feckless minister than the noble bishop in *Les Misérables*. In far too many instances, guys just can't seem to get it together, while women, on the other hand, always can, and are regularly portrayed as superior to men in intelligence, competency and sophistication. Our children notice.

Television programs such as *Married with Children*, *Men Behaving Badly*, *The Simpsons*, and *How I Met Your Mother* have often depicted men in ways that most of us baby boomers never knew as we were growing up. Movies and television (programs and commercials) have striven to reshape the sexual norms. For example, in *Queer Eye for the Straight Guy*, one of the early programs in this endeavor, the portrayal of heterosexual men brought this response from anthropologist and author Lionel Tiger: "Heteromales are the last group it is acceptable to bash as a class…The program is degraded and degrading." This pattern has continued apace. Now that same-sex marriage has been legalized, one wonders if advertisers will continue to depict the buffoonery of the "husband" (but that begs the obvious question: "which one?").

The great respect I have for many of the women in my life is based upon their inherent dignity, as well as their demonstrable virtue and wisdom. Since the former is a given and the latter available for the choosing, it is clear that women do not need—and should not want—men to decline in order for them to advance.

When we think of male actors from an earlier age, did they seem unsure of themselves? They did not. While each certainly did stupid things off-camera, their public and private identities were not associated with those behaviors. Growing up, I regularly saw men portrayed as responsible leaders in their families, as in shows such as *Father Knows Best*. Having 27 years' experience as a father, I can confirm that that statement is not always true. But the point is that men, especially fathers, were generally edified and presented as respectable figures. Today that portrayal is, sadly, rare.

The giants of an earlier age of the silver screen and TV dwarf the modern male actors, who seem to be oversized boys bereft of traditional masculinity. Dr. Marcia Sirota, of the Ruthless Compassion Institute, has expressed the concern that too many of our modern leading men are like her Ken doll of Barbie fame. They behave as if they, like Ken, have nothing between their legs, referring to the "…epidemic of emasculated men in the movies today…" And that "it's far more likely that an American audience today would see full frontal male nudity than a demonstration of genuine masculinity. On screen, the actual apparatus is apparently less threatening than a representation of genuine masculine power and individuality."

Several television shows of the fifties and sixties had titles that began with *The Adventures of…*or portrayed competent men in all walks of life. Boys wanted to emulate these characters because there was much to admire. Generally, the men in those shows were sure of their place in the universe, could handle themselves in virtually any situation, and were often gentlemanly.

Conversely, it is difficult for us to imagine most boys and men eager to emulate the males in programs such as *The Big Bang Theory* or *Glee*. Mention of these shows is not intended to be a denigration of male dancers, gamer geeks or brainy boys who don't play sports. It is only to emphasize the point that most boys would not typically want to emulate guys who are riddled with anxieties, uncertain of their gender, and full of sarcastic humor at somebody else's expense. And any effort to find traditional morality—on any show—would very often lead to frustration, since profanity and vulgarity have been steadily advanced while the heroic portrayals of men recede further into the archives.

The Changing Media, and Its Effects

The website www.TVdads.com indicates that from 1950 through 2012, there have been 272 shows with single fathers playing a leading role. A closer look reveals that beginning in the 1980s, the main reason for their singleness had changed. Prior to that decade, death of the wife was the reason, but once the baby boomer children became parents, the reason was much more likely to be divorce and, lately, homosexuality. Strikingly, there was only one show during the first thirty years in which divorce was the reason for the singleness.

The research into the influence television has had on the culture has yielded mixed results over the past 10-15 years. But parents don't have to risk their children's well-being as part of a grand experiment until those results become definite (if they ever do), by allowing them excessive exposure to media of all kinds. Data from a 2002 report by Cope-Farrar and Kunkel indicate how programs emphasize sexual promiscuity while minimizing chastity or modesty. In their report "Happily Never After: How Hollywood Favors Adultery and Promiscuity Over Marital Intimacy on Prime Time Broadcast Television," the Parents Television Council describes a 2003 survey of American parents in which nearly 90 percent expressed concern about TV encouraging the loss of their children's innocence and their premature engagement in sexual activity. Studies done for the Rand Corporation, published in the journals *Pediatrics* and *The Journal of Personal and Social Psychology*, showed that the onset of adolescent sexual activity could be predicted by the amount of exposure to media sexual content, and that this behavioral change could be explained by self-perception about how they could confidently handle sexual situations, and by perceiving that sexual activity in their peer group is normal. Still, these findings were mostly predictive rather than definitive.

Numerous wide-ranging and comprehensive studies have identified clear patterns of "ill-being" (as opposed to "well-being") in those children, pre-teens and teenagers that had *significant* media exposure (which probably means virtually every person in that age group). One such study, published in 2014 in *Computers and Human Behavior*, helped to demonstrate this pattern. In "Media and technology use predicts ill-being among children, preteens and teenagers independent of the negative health impacts of exercise and eating habits," author L. D. Rosen found that excessive media consumption predicts significant problems in psychological health, behavioral issues, attentiveness and physical health in at least *50% of teenagers*.

Today, the big problem is the little screen: the smartphone. In early 2018, according to the Wall Street Journal[7], investor groups made an unusual and dramatic move by sending a letter to Apple, in which they expressed concern about the iPhone's impact on children's health. Specifically, the concern focused on the potential for children to become addicted to their iPhones, and how the technology company could develop software to help parents regain some control over the time limits children would be able to use the phone. This correspondence was significantly driven by worries over the device's ill effects on the mental health of children, particularly skyrocketing depression and suicide. Jean M. Twenge explores the problem in much more depth, as the subtitle of her new book makes clear. In *iGen: Why Today's Super-Connected Kids Are Growing Up Less Rebellious, More Tolerant, Less Happy—and Completely Unprepared for Adulthood—and What That Means for the Rest of Us*, Twenge paints a gloomy picture of the decreasing *interpersonal* connectedness among those born between 1995 and 2012. For them, the chief form of communication is texting with that phone in the solitude of their rooms rather than talking into it—*and then listening*—let alone being in that room with friends or doing something outside with them so they can then share their experiences. And when the uncommon person-to-person experience actually happens, it hurts to realize that your "friend" is not really listening to you, but is instead busily texting another friend.

What is the obvious conclusion? Parents must reassert their authority, and act intentionally and purposefully to control their children's use of technology and social media (that assumes they at one time had that authority). I wonder if the most striking aspect of the news story above isn't the proclaimed need by parents for an outside entity to exert that control. If true, then the hierarchy at home is out of sync! Parents should reduce their children's exposure to media, control the media to which their children are exposed and, most importantly, increase the time they interact—imaginatively—with their children. In our family's early years, we regularly gathered in the living room and listened to

---

[7] https://www.wsj.com/articles/iphones-and-children-are-a-toxic-pair-say-two-big-apple-investors-1515358834

audiobook mysteries and dramas, allowing each of us to imagine the scenes and then discuss it afterwards. It was great fun, and I miss it.

It Takes All Kinds

We should neither expect nor want every boy to grow up and become a Rifleman or a Lone Ranger. Creative artists, thoughtful philosophers, and charitable religious individuals have taken their own heroes' journeys and greatly enhanced our lives. But the media all too often portray boys and men in ways that were virtually never admired throughout our history or the history of any culture.

There certainly is no guarantee that every boy mentored by a man of courage will himself become courageous, let alone have a successful life. And there are certainly good men among us who had no such model in their fathers, but who became just and charitable because of heroic mothers. But it is very likely that men of virtue, over the ages and in our time, were most likely formed from boyhood with the help of at least one good man.

It may be too late for some, but I believe there's hope for most. That hope lies in the determination by their fathers, or other caring men, to be the guardians and mentors so desperately needed by boys—and not the dimwitted, outwitted or misfit TV dads.

CHAPTER 7

The Dating Game

*You can discover more about a person in an hour
of play than in a year of conversation.*

—Plato

IN THE UNITED STATES, THERE are approximately seventy million baby boomers, those born between 1946 and 1964, which form the predominant population of parents. For most, if not all of them, *play* meant leaving the house for outdoor activities, either by themselves or with neighborhood friends, but always with their boundless imagination.

In his 2008 book, *Children at Play—An American History*, Howard P. Chudacoff describes the Boomer era as "the golden age of unstructured play," sharing themes of spontaneity, fun, and friendship formation, generally outdoors, to provide many opportunities to test oneself while interacting with each other. Chudacoff describes a crucial aspect of this joyous venture, saying that play should help children develop and assert autonomy. He cites the work of many psychologists to form the basis of this development, and among them is Erik Erikson's work showing that play helps children transition from the world of home to the world of peers.

Linda Perlstein, author of *Not Much Just Chillin': The Hidden Lives of Middle Schoolers* writes, "Youth is a species that hungers for freedom as it lives on reliance." So, even while youngsters need adults for the basic necessities of life, they strive to be free of that dependence. Independence must happen as the boy enters the unknown, having crossed the first threshold in his hero's journey. Independent play is supposed to prepare him for that.

Shlomo Ariel and Irene Sever, writing in the journal *Play and Culture*, point out that children at play—be they in foreign lands or the U.S.—spontaneously form mini societies in which children—on their own—learn about hierarchy, sharing, and membership.

And while humorist Robert Paul Smith jokingly states "children and grownups are natural enemies," it is often true that children rebel against adults because they want to have their own world of fun. Supporting this, L. Joseph Stone and Joseph Church describe the independence of children at play as "a special culture, with its own traditional games and mythical lore... transmitted virtually intact from one childhood generation to the next... over a period of centuries, *with no help from adults and often in spite of them* (emphasis added)."

Children must have the opportunity to become skillful at managing their thoughts, emotions, and actions when finding themselves in a variety of situations through unstructured and unsupervised play. But ever since baby boomers became parents, much has changed in the play of American children—particularly for boys. This is reflected in a relatively new addition to our language: the "playdate."

BAD DATES

I recall the first time I heard this term. Kevin and Maureen were approximately nine and five years old, respectively, when new neighbors moved into the development. Lucas and Julia (not their real names) were approximately the same ages, and I was looking forward to all of them forming good friendships from many hours of play. But the parents of these children defined "play" and "friendship" much differently than I.

One day my wife told me she had spoken with Lucas' mother, and that the two of them had arranged a playdate for Kevin and Lucas, to be held at Lucas' house under the supervision of Lucas' mother. I thought, with some consternation,

"What's a playdate? Boys don't need dates to play. Why can't they just go outside...and play?" I wondered why Lucas' parents thought they needed to coordinate this, and, more importantly, why the boys would need to be supervised.

Unfortunately, the playdate was to be my next indoctrination into the new parenting model, and a very unpleasant one. I don't know when this change became the norm, as that experience was the first I'd heard of it. But I soon learned that all the mothers knew the term, and that there was, by necessity, a feminine influence.

Admittedly, in some situations, the playdate is the only way for children to get together, perhaps because of distances too great for them to walk. And although family norms are changing, mothers still tend to be home more often than fathers. But rather than just drop off the child, the parent often remains and collaborates with the other parent to organize, supervise, and intrude during playtime. The playdate phenomenon has certainly been understandable, driven as it has been by a ratings-hungry news media's alarmist reporting, one that has shaped parents' minds into thinking every neighborhood is riddled with evildoers.

Katrina Kenison, author of *Mitten Strings for God: Reflections for Mothers in a Hurry*, described how boredom benefitted today's parents during their own childhood, but notes they are not allowing the same for their children: "Left to our own amusements, we found resources that we didn't know we had... These were valuable lessons—and I fear that our own busy, well-entertained children may not ever have the chance to learn them. Inventiveness and self-reliance are being scheduled right out of them."

In her article "The Creativity Crisis," educational psychologist Kyung Hee Kim, of the College of William and Mary, describes a steady decline in creative thinking in American children over the past forty years, particularly in grades K–6. Among the reasons she gives for this decline are:

- Decreased free time for unstructured physical activity,
- Highly structured (academic) activities,
- Excessive interference from technology, and
- Insufficient time with the undivided attention of parents.

It seems that Kim is describing Lucas' family, and too many others, a situation that negatively impacted Kevin because he was always interested in spontaneous outdoor play. I became very irritated about the new world of playdates—and with its parents.

In this world it is parents and not children who settle disagreements and coerce agreements, thereby depriving boys (and girls) the opportunity to learn how to deal with conflict and gain the confidence and independence that grows from that. They will learn from their parents that they can handle neither their disputes nor themselves. One result is too many boys remaining as heroes-in-waiting, because they are either unable to answer the call, refuse the call or cannot hear that call because everything is organized and supervised with no need for imagination, resourcefulness, and grit. So it is understandable that Kevin was upset with me on his first walk home by himself, when I initially shadowed him in the car.

Plato believed play and education, throughout life, should often be intertwined for the good of the community and benefit of the nation. That seems partly reasonable, particularly if there is legitimate play allowed both in and out of school. However, the playful world of children should not be used as a formal educational tool. Writing about the changes in both toys and games, Chudacoff asserts, "The emphasis now is on educational toys, which allow adults and schools to infiltrate childhood."

With technology having become increasingly part of the toy experience, parents should be mindful of the advice of child psychologist Stanley Greenspan: "The value of a toy is proportional to the degree that it invites imagination and creativity." As if reinforcing that point, Joan Almon, Coordinator for the Alliance for Childhood, relates a conversation between two girls describing the value of their dolls. "One girl had an electronically-enhanced doll and boasted: 'My doll can say 500 words!' The other girl was holding an old-fashioned cloth doll and countered: 'My doll can say anything I want her to say.'" One girl's play was passive observance, with a brain only slightly involved, while the other's was active participant, fully engaging her brain to *become* that doll and bring it to life.

Unfortunately for Julia, Lucas' sister, her dolls were not able to speak in any manner or form. That's because her mother wanted them, not for playing, but to remain in the original boxes as keepsake dolls, ultimately preventing her child from receiving the riches in imagination and memories for Julia to bring her friends "to life." Mother fully controlled the dolls—and tried earnestly to do the same with her children.

Play Should Involve Risk

Today's parents exaggerate the injury risk. In her paper titled "Children's Risky Play from an Evolutionary Perspective: The Anti-Phobic Effects of Thrilling Experiences," researcher Ellen Sandseter of Norway writes, "In modern western society there is a growing focus on the safety of children in all areas, including situations involving playing. An exaggerated safety focus of children's play is problematic because...they might need challenges and varied stimulation to develop normally, both physically and mentally." It seems reasonable to look at our "safe spaces" in colleges, and link the perceived need for them to parents' overemphasizing safety in their children's youth.

Even rubber surfacing playgrounds doesn't seem to have made much of a difference in the real world. David Ball, professor of Risk Management at Middlesex University, analyzed UK injury statistics and found that, as in the United States, there was no clear trend over time. "The advent of all these special surfaces for playgrounds has contributed very little, if anything at all, to the safety of children." He believes kids don't perceive a risk, and become inattentive to technique.

Another factor in this risk avoidance is the high divorce rate, largely because boys suffer without dad's roughhousing. His type of play helps train the child to maintain emotional equilibrium in a variety of stimulated environments.

In a 2004 report titled "An Investigation of the Status of Outdoor Play," Professor Rhonda Clements, then of Hofstra University, surveyed more than eight hundred mothers throughout rural, suburban, and urban America, asking for their comparison of the amount of vigorous outdoor playtime they had as children versus how much their children had. The contrast is startling because their children had significantly less. It is also disturbing because of the negative implications for the children's health and potential impact upon their future and society's. Clements makes clear that outdoor play offers great opportunities to help children mature physically, cognitively, and emotionally in a natural environment, but that today's children have become markedly passive, with mothers worrying about harm to their children. However, the crime and injury statistics from sources such as the FBI and municipal organizations clearly don't support these concerns. The mothers have made very clear their understanding of the importance of this type of play, yet their children are comparatively sedentary. Clements describes this as "a vast disconnection."

In another study completed several years ago with fourth graders, the researchers found significant but unsurprising results. "If you compare children who have had recess with those who have not had recess, the children who didn't have recess were more fidgety and less on task," said Olga Jarrett, a University of Georgia early childhood education professor who has completed extensive research on the recess issue. "I suspect," she continues, "that a lot of what we are seeing in terms of hyperactivity in kids may be related to the inappropriateness of the school day for children's physical needs. When you look at a school day with no breaks, you have to wonder how an adult would function in the same situation." Well, one result in adults as well as children is obesity, and its associated problems.

The American Academy of Pediatricians wrote a position statement in late 2012 in which they described the scientific reasons why daily recess benefits both the minds and bodies of children. Apparently not enough people paid attention to that group, as new evidence shows that too many adolescents are sedentary. The National Center for Health Statistics released a study in early 2014 showing that only one teenager out of four gets one hour of activity a day. And since people typically overestimate their good qualities, the true result is more likely to be even lower activity levels.

During my formative years, my friends and I were active in ways similar to our ancestors, only with modern ideas. So we formed high-powered rifles from branches or hand grenades from rocks, scaled to the highest peaks of construction sites in order to be king of the hill, and then rolled all the way down to the bottom of the foundation.

When girls made mud pies, the high-spirited boys would run and then leap as high as possible in order to land on them, splatting mud far and wide. We weren't trying to be mean-spirited; we simply saw them as irresistible targets, ones that, when hit, would provide untold fun—at least for us. That's just biology driving the behavior of a normal boy. This biology got me into big trouble when I was approximately eleven years old, but taught me some valuable lessons I've never forgotten.

Michael and the Knife

During this particular summer day, my neighbor and I were wandering around and becoming a little bored, a potentially troubling combination for most boys and especially when Michael was involved. My parents didn't like Michael because of his notorious troublemaking, mischief that was at a much higher level than mine. One time he nearly blew off his hand and part of my face because he had held onto an ignited cherry bomb a bit too long. Something within me made me turn suddenly away, right before the blast. That "something" was apparently missing from Michael's brain, perhaps because he had very little guidance from his father and older brothers. The image of him screaming, while running around in circles holding his bloodied and maimed hand, is unforgettable. Sometimes a boy gets bored with nothing to do, and makes poor choices. I made one of those choices, and soon proved my parents correct about the effects of a bad influence.

On this occasion, Michael let me borrow a knife owned by his older brother, who was away serving in the Navy during the Vietnam conflict. It was big, shiny and looked very sharp. Up to that point in my life, the only knife I was allowed to hold was a simple Cub Scout penknife or one only meant to be used at the dinner table. For the first few seconds holding it, I was unaware of anything else in life. The thick, hardwood handle was contoured for a better grip. The ten-inch blade glimmered in the sunlight when I moved it, and seemed to be perfectly weighted. It looked sharper and cooler than any knife I had ever seen, and I was therefore eager to put it to good and honorable use. But I was about to learn how such a valuable tool could be so misused, and bring dishonor to the user. At the time, it wasn't clear to me that the frontal lobe of either Michael's brain or mine was fully matured, giving a perfect reason to keep knives and many other things out of the hands of boys.

It was Michael's idea to skin the bark from a nearby street-side shade tree. He didn't say why he selected this tree. Perhaps it was because the trunk diameter was relatively small and the bark thin, making it very manageable for our tools and for us. Or maybe it was because the tree was not on either Michael's or my property. We never considered the possibility that someone owned this tree, as it was between the sidewalk and the street. The plan seemed like a good one to me. I just wanted to have at that tree!

We proceeded to work the sharpened steel on our respective sides of the tree, straining our bodies to reach as high as possible while watching the skin come off and feeling little resistance. We were surprisingly careful not to maim ourselves—or each other. *"Man, what a cool knife!"* I remember thinking at the time. My eyes were wide with delight at how sharp that blade was, and how quickly the bark came off. It was easy to imagine the tree being a giant potato, with us eagerly peeling away the bark in order to see, for the first time, what lay underneath. The blade did my bidding, almost as if it knew that it was fulfilling its purpose in life. Each boy assisted the other in climbing higher so that they could skin all the way up to the relatively high branch line.

My cohort and I were amazed to discover the underside of bark, never before having known anything but the grayish brown colors on the surface. It was bald, juicy and a creamy white, almost exactly like a spud. And there must have been an inviting aroma because I stretched out my tongue and gave it a big lick—much to my regret. The gagging that quickly followed the awful feeling in my mouth lasted quite a while, which of course resulted in Michael laughing so hard that he almost wet himself. But I would soon have the last laugh.

A tree without its bark is extremely slick, and we quickly realized that no individual attempt by either to scale its heights would be successful. But Michael's inquisitive nature got the better of him, and so he insisted on going higher. After I recovered from the awful taste, I clasped my hands together tightly in order to help Michael get to the highest point possible, unaware of the joy that would soon follow—*for me*. So I crouched and braced myself, at which point Michael placed one foot into my hands, one hand on my shoulder and the other hand on the tree. The grit on his shoes dug painfully into my skin when he twisted during his maneuvering. On the count of three, Michael pushed off at the same time that I lifted, and he shot up to the highest branch he could grab—but only with his left hand since his right was holding the knife. He made approximately three strokes with the knife before fatigue quickly set in, at which point his grip began to fail. When he could no longer hold on, he wrapped both arms around the tree, making him my first encounter with a tree-hugger.

But almost immediately his eyes revealed the panic of his mind's realization that he'd made a mistake. I'm not sure what amazed me more during his rapid and uncontrolled downward slide: the repeated *"Ow, ow, ow!"* when his genitals hit every branch nub that we hadn't removed, or the burning smell coming from the same region due to the friction from tree rubbing pants. But it didn't matter. We both hit the ground, but only I was laughing. Within seconds the burn from that friction reached deeper into his nether regions, causing an amazing change in his voice—a change that brought the name *Michelle* to mind rather than Michael.

In his famous autobiography *Confessions*, Augustine painfully lamented the time he stole pears from a nearby orchard. To many readers, his remorse could seem wildly misplaced. After all, many crimes have resulted from the desire to taste the sweet forbidden fruit. However, his theft was *not* for the enjoyment of the fruit, but simply for the sake of stealing—which worsened the sin. My humble confession is that, while I should have known better, I was simply thrilled to feel and see the performance of that knife cutting away the bark. I wasn't thinking of sin, and therein lay my problem. Looking back, it seems that wonderful knife had what the Greeks referred to as *telos*—a purpose or end—not just to be or to exist like Julia's dolls, but to *do* and then *become*. The tree became the object upon which the knife would fulfill its purpose.

Not long after returning home, I heard my mother answer the telephone, and all I could hear were her comments, tinged with an ominous tone, ending with, "I'll send him over now with his brother." As it happened, the tree had an owner, and Mrs. Baldwin had apparently looked out her front room window and saw us just as we were leaving the scene.

My father, a big believer in habeas corpus, instructed my oldest brother, Joe, to walk me over to face my accuser. Thinking back, I can easily recall some of Joe's own mischiefs, and I have learned of more over the years. So having him escort me to the crime scene was akin to having Frank James escort his brother Jesse to the courtroom. We were still a distance away when Mrs. Baldwin turned toward us. Her steel blue eyes locked onto mine and bore into me. My shame made it impossible to maintain the connection, and I looked down. The tree, it turned out, had sentimental value to her.

"Why did you do this?" she asked in both anger and pain. "My husband planted this tree for me and our son!" Had there been a hole in the ground, I would have crawled into it in disgrace at being such a scoundrel at so young an age. But with immediate intensity, I decided I would not have a life of villainy, and would change my ways.

"I'm sorry," I whispered through a tight throat; and I meant it. I'm not sure she believed me, because she just turned her back on me and walked down her gravel driveway, turning slowly to enter her house. Her great disappointment in mankind was easy to sense, and I felt badly for having caused it. I wanted to plead my case of ignorance and no malice aforethought, and that I would be forever changed. But what little wisdom I possessed kept my mouth shut, and she probably went to her grave knowing nothing else about me other than this experience.

Amazingly, upon my return home, my father's only reaction was to firmly tell me how our choices and associations could impact our lives. I never forgot this experience; it taught me to think before I act, and that my actions could simultaneously produce joy and sorrow. I also learned the impact and value of a firm but gentle admonishment, when least expected, and the teachable moment that could follow. That was the last time I hung around with Michael. Unfortunately, it wasn't the last time I would use poor judgment.

If my parents had supervised and orchestrated all my activities and only allowed organized playdates, then a tree may have been saved. But that was not how parents typically behaved—and I would not have learned the attendant lessons that began my transformation to manhood, and helped me to be a better parent. Since Lucas and Julia were the only friends in the neighborhood that matched Kevin and Maureen for age and sex, we were forced into the playdate world. But I couldn't wait to leave it.

When adults intrude into their children's play, they deprive them of the formative benefits of many learning experiences, and lower the chance the culture will benefit from the emergence of a new hero. Parents need to give their sons the training, discipline, and freedom to be able and willing to improve the chances that they will answer the call—and become one.

CHAPTER 8

Heroic Warriors, or Worriers?

*People are so busy lengthening their lives with
exercise they don't have time to live them.*

—Jonathan Miller

*And I grew afraid of everything around me—afraid
of the air, afraid of the night.*

—Guy de Maupassant

Regardless of one's age, the hero's journey is difficult, implying an inherent risk. For fathers, the perils they face are the seemingly mundane activities of building lives—those of their children and themselves.

Men that have regular interaction with boys, particularly their sons, have the opportunity to provide the Supernatural Aid referred to by Campbell, and prepare their charges for life's hazards. It is the best way. And a very good reason for doing this is because each boy *will* be tested: by nature, events at school, and interactions with people of all ages throughout all stages of life. This provides both planned and random teaching opportunities. In the first, both the man and the boy know that a lesson is being taught about a particular aspect of life. That may be about sports, relationships or virtues. The second opportunity is simply the unconscious learning that takes place when the boy interacts with a good man or sees the man interact with others.

But the timing and environment of the lesson must be an opportune one, or else the lesson will be lost. This I learned one evening during Kevin's senior year in high school, as he came into my bedroom after (presumably) finishing his homework. I was relaxing in my bed for a few minutes, aided by the soft glow from the street lamp as the room's only illumination. Having had, at the time, 18 years of experience with my son, I'd become fairly good at knowing his mannerisms—but I didn't anticipate this one. When he flopped down onto the mattress he uttered a groan, one that suggested the tension of the day was being released from his muscles and which therefore opened the door to a state of deep relaxation. Our fatigue allowed by a brief burst of floppy-limbed wrestling, and our remaining energy allowed but a little banter; and it was at this time that I chose to wax philosophical about life in general, and his future in particular. After several minutes of enjoying what I thought to be his undivided and rapt attention at my sage advice, I became aware of another sound: his slow and rhythmic breathing. That's when I looked over and found him deep in dreamland, and wondered at which brilliant point of mine did his brainwave shift from the relaxed alpha into the deep slumber of delta.

Still, when we get it right, no lesson is learned better than the one in which we have become fully engaged—come what may. The gallantry we exhibit is especially significant if it is in response to a challenge of one's historical or, more importantly, one's assumed limits, such that success can only come if one exceeds them. And though the resultant victory may only be moral, such as in Thomas More's sacrifice, time often shows that this is the kind that counts in the end and what William Ernest Henley seems to indicate in this passage from *Invictus*:

> In the fell clutch of circumstance
> I have not winced nor cried aloud
> Under the bludgeonings of chance
> My head is bloody, but unbowed.

I recall when Kevin courageously stood his ground during his first fight at the family barbecue. I don't know what thoughts, if any, he had going into this altercation, or if he was just reacting. However, I do know that his many wrestling matches with me up to that point were helpful, as he exerted great effort at trying to beat me. But, psychologically, going against an unknown boy in front of other peers is entirely different, and was a new experience for him. This was a test for him based upon an important concept.

A boy's limits are typically based upon the amount of confidence he has in his own capability of doing something, which, up to that particular point, he had never done. Right growth toward manhood is based upon a boy's response to circumstances that push him off his path, and how soon he returns after having either chosen or been forced to leave. Further, his willingness to test himself, to acknowledge any failure of character or will, and to courageously right himself so he may continue, ultimately results in success. This doesn't mean he gets the prize simply for participating, because that devalues the measurable reality of the greater competitive achievement of his competitor, and of improving each time. However, it can mean he is heroic. Whether or not a boy achieves that title in all his experiences, he should at least be given the necessary training to make the best choice and take the best stand. Instead of boys focusing on their "own private pursuits to the detriment of the common cause," as Thomas More described, their freedom of choice should be formed with others in mind, rather than just in the name of the modern trinity: me, myself, and I.

As Joseph Campbell showed, legends are made and written about those who, like More, adhered unwaveringly to moral truths because of a properly formed conscience. While martyrdom is unlikely, a cost is still often paid when choosing to do the right thing. But today's moral relativism of "It's all good" and "I have my truth, you have your truth" avoids those costs—temporarily. The risk-averse behavior that allows it and results from it suggests there are fewer boys on the threshold of heroism. After all, what need is there for that fortitude if everything is relative and we can each make up our own truth and define words however we want? One result of this cultural change is that there will be fewer men with the stuff of which legends are made, because those legends were heroic in defense of near-universally recognized truths. To avoid that, children must be properly formed and allowed to take risks.

GERMS ARE NOT THE BIGGEST THREAT

The protective behavior of parents noted in the previous chapter reflects their vigilance about many imagined threats. It is possible that advertising has contributed to this phenomenon, as suggested by Cornell University researchers in the *Journal of Communication*. Led by Professor Jeff Niederdeppe, their studies, published in 2007 with a follow-up in 2013, showed that alarmist news reporting about disease has a tendency "to cultivate the belief that everything causes cancer."

Some concern is justified because bad things and bad people exist. But that's been true for all of human history. Today, way too many believe that danger is always lurking, ready to pounce if we don't scrub ourselves every minute, take a hundred pills, or hover over our children - even into adulthood. For these worriers, safety is paramount and all germs and risks should be avoided. Therefore, every shopping cart handle, doorknob and TV remote should be sanitized before we grab it, despite evidence from the Centers for Disease Control and Prevention (CDC) that these cleaners risk the development of bacteria resistance, immune system impairment, and allergic tendencies—and do not work as advertised.

We've developed so much fear and worry about so many bad things presumed to be looming around us, only to find in the end that Mark Twain was right when he said, "I have spent most of my life worrying about things that never happened." This dread has changed our approach to so many experiences we enjoyed as kids.

NOT HALLOWEEN GOBLINS...

The traditional Halloween scene rarely happens anymore because parents believe it too dangerous. The false tales of poisoned candy and razor-filled apples were perpetrated and perpetuated by the media, and parents believed what they heard. Before I went out, my parents simply told me to not eat any fruit, cookies, or open candy until they were checked at home. It wasn't until I got older that I realized this "checking" usually meant my father would try some of the candy—just to be sure. And the apple scare was amazing, because no one I knew ever kept the fruit.

The *Washington Post* reported in their 1993 Halloween edition, "In the ten years the National Confectioners Association has run its Halloween Hotline, the group has yet to verify an instance of tampering." Their spokesman asserted, "These myths become truisms." Furthermore, Joel Best, professor of sociology at Cal State University, Fresno, investigated seventy-eight reports of these crimes from 1958 to 1988 and found virtually all were pranks—done by kids. He found reports of only two deaths of children, one of which was accidental and the other a murder of a boy by his father. The Associated Press reported in 2012 that there has been no evidence of even one child's death as a result of eating tainted candy or a razor-filled apple, or from being murdered by a predator.

But many fictions die hard, or not at all. So despite overwhelming evidence to the contrary, parents cart their little goblins all over, and then shadow them from their vehicles. It became another chapter in the story of overinvolved parents. The irony for today's children is that the only immediate danger they face during trick-or-treating is from being hit by a car because of the traffic-filled streets. Of course, the combination of massive amounts of sugar calories and being transported by car contribute to the much larger danger to children: obesity. The risk of their being kidnapped during one night of fun or any other night is, according to statistics, minimal. FBI records show the classic kidnapping for even one overnight is a rare event. National statistics for 2009 show only 115 kidnappings—out of seventy-five million children—by a stranger for more than one day. Most missing children are runaways from abusive or broken homes.

This information brings two compelling realizations to mind: the risk of kidnapping is rare, and children don't run away from good homes with loving parents. When abductions do occur, it most likely involves a parent as part of a custody-related problem.

Not Even the Bicycle...

Another rite of passage through childhood is learning to ride a bicycle. One reason for this is the thrill experienced from learning to control oneself in an unstable environment with ever-increasing speed—at the risk of falling. It is a lot like life. You can be rolling along and having a good time, then without warning lose control or be pushed off balance—and then, crash. Generally, the hurt is from skinned legs with an occasional broken bone, but rarely anything serious. However, today's parents want to eliminate that risk, a desire that is impossible to realize.

An example of this desire was made evident many years ago, on a day when Kevin was outside with a neighbor's daughter as each was learning to master their bicycle. That child's father and I were walking a distance behind them when my son started to teeter away from equilibrium and toward the inevitable crash. As he moved his leg out to break his fall, the other father sprang forward and dove in a failed attempt to catch my son, putting him further off balance and making matters worse.

After determining Kevin was OK, I wondered how I was measuring up as a father. My first thought was that I should have been the one trying to stop his fall. However, I quickly realized that not only was I not close enough to help, but also that my son hadn't needed me to dive in an attempt to "save" him. Stopping his fall of a couple of feet would have prevented him from learning a valuable lesson, one that we all have learned or should have: you fall, your brush yourself off, and then you get back on the saddle. The damage comes years later when children teeter in adulthood and daddy isn't there to save them. Overprotective parents are hurting our children.

According to 2009 data from the National Highway Traffic Safety Administration, the number of bicycle fatalities for every million riders is just two, and the average age of the deceased is twenty-nine. The injury rate is well below 1 percent, and of that group, the average age is thirty-nine. Although statistics suggest wearing a helmet will lower the risk, that risk is already very low. I support the practice of having young children wear a helmet, because it is a minor inconvenience to protect against a potentially serious injury. But I oppose the dread and fear of danger too many parents impart to their children—be it about riding a bike or playing outside.

The Real Danger

The behavior described above is a far cry from the practices of various indigenous cultures I have researched. The Amazon Indian tribes have long known that for elders to train young boys into manhood, it is important to have them experience pain in a controlled environment and learn how to respond to it. In this way, they will be able to respond better to the pain they'll encounter in the *uncontrolled* experiment called "life." To our modern ears, this seems harsh and excessive. But their reasoning points to the purpose of this training, and something all parents should teach: "If you know neither suffering nor great exertion, then your life will have no meaning." This is another example of purposeful and intentional upbringing.

The actions taken by the overly protective father described in the above bicycle incident proved to be tragically hypocritical, because he ended up leaving his family to start a new one. He turned out to be not quite the protector he imagined himself to be. The hurt his children would have felt from a fall off their bikes would have lasted perhaps a few hours, and a cut a few days, but that is nothing compared with a lifetime of pain the father caused by the destruction of his family and abandonment of his children. If he had striven to protect his marriage with the same vigor he used with my son, he would still be my neighbor—with his family intact.

Parents go to extremes looking outward to perceived dangers all around them, perhaps thinking well of themselves for this vigilance. Yet divorce or abandonment would rightly make the children turn on us and cry out, "Hypocrites! You're so worried about us being hurt by falls, germs, and strangers, when it is *you* who are the biggest threat of all!"

So Halloween candy, germs and bicycle riding help make up a real life, and are not the threats we've made them out to be. They help form us on whichever journey we take. But if we adults would take just one look in the mirror, we would see the real threat to our children—we've made them worriers, not warriors, insecure about their place in the world, insisting on safe spaces and unable to take their hero's journey.

CHAPTER 9

Schooling Our Boys

*One of the greatest problems…is that many
are schooled but few are educated.*

—THOMAS MORE

Wisdom starts with owning up to ignorance.

—PLATO

NOT LONG AFTER A BOY begins school, and throughout his academic career, he will find himself involved in a wide variety of situations and with a similar array of personalities. His behavior during many of those engagements will help define him, and while some will be mundane, others will present him with the opportunity to become the hero, villain, or victim. Since he is a rational being, his response to these situations is, naturally, a free will choice, but the correct choice is heavily dependent upon how he has been formed. Thomas More asserted that the goal of education is to "train the soul in virtue," leading to understanding goodness and excellence, as well as truth. Heroic behavior assumes virtue. And parental guidance should provide the foundation to help make those choices virtuous, while formal education, including its discipline, must support them to help ensure these decisions are reasoned throughout the child's life.

By the time Kevin was nearing school age, my wife and I had become increasingly aware of problems boys had been having in school, and eventually learned about their probable causes. One reason was ignorance about differences in the structure and function of the brains of boys and girls, and how these brains respond differently to the usual curricula and teaching methods (geared more toward girls' brains than boys'). Another reason is that policies based upon political correctness, and its zero tolerance offshoot, disproportionately impact boys. Perhaps the most important factor is troubles at home, a problem I never thought Kevin would have to face.

Over the past several decades, these challenges have occurred with much more frequency, and statistics related to their education are troubling:

- Boys read far fewer books than girls.
- 70% of all D and F grades go to boys.
- Boys account for up to 90% of classroom discipline referrals, and have higher dropout rates. Approximately 70% of learning disability diagnoses are given to boys.

Rather than assist me in helping my son become the man God designed him to be, I came to believe the public educational system would likely be a major trial on his journey.

The Boy Brain

According to groups such as The Boys Project, and researchers such as Dr. Michael Gurian and Dr. Leonard Sax (leaders in the single-sex education movement), elementary school curricula reflects an inadequate understanding of the brain differences between boys and girls, and their classrooms therefore tend not to be "boy-friendly." Boys often report that they don't belong in the classroom, and that school is for girls.

Modern technology has shown how differently the brains of the two sexes work while engaged in the same tasks. According to Dr. Gurian, author of *Successful Single-Sex Classrooms,* "girls process and respond to classroom information faster," and boys are "more apt to respond impulsively and, in general, to think less before they act."

A common theme in reports on boys' lagging academic performance is the dearth of their physical activity. Interestingly, this not only refers to recess or physical education, but also to regular classes as well. Boys must sit still, despite their testosterone-driven need for movement. And while sitting still, they must then struggle with tasks based solely on cognitive and emotive models, rather than incorporating their needs for both physical action and competition. Carla Hannaford, neurophysiologist and author of *Smart Moves: Why Learning Is Not All in Your Head*, asserts that movement and play more fully engage the brain and enhance learning. As I delved deeper into this research, I enjoyed fond recollections of how my teachers generously allowed activity times for my classmates and me.

In our brain, the cerebellum acts as a relay mechanism between our muscles and other brain areas, and it is significantly larger in males than in females. Dr. Gurian refers to this as our "doing center of the brain" and goes on to say, "Boys often learn better when their bodies are in motion. Sitting still can frustrate the male, causing a boy to exhibit behavior that can appear disruptive, and land him in the principal's office because he can't sit still when he's really responding to his biological needs." Knowing the problems I had in elementary school, it seemed he was describing me.

In *Boys Adrift*, Dr. Sax comments on the significance of these findings: "When we compare a 6-year-old girl with a 6-year-old boy, we find that the average 6-year-old boy can sit still, be quiet, and pay attention for only about half as long as the average 6-year-old girl. He may be sitting still and being quiet, but he is not paying attention."

Some would argue that school has always required boys to sit still and be quiet. While this may have been true during many of the classes, it would have been required in the context of a very different day in a boy's life. Up until recently, a boy's day would be much more active; kindergarten would have begun more gradually; tolerance would have been greater than zero; and his father would have been a guiding force in his life.

Anthropologist Lionel Tiger, author of *Decline of Males: The First Look at an Unexpected New World for Men and Women*, wrote about "male original sin." During one interview in 2004, Tiger was asked if men had become the second sex. "There certainly is an attitudinal factor…so that almost anything males do is (therefore) questionable and potentially dangerous. The schools have become anti-male, though the disastrous decline of male performance compared with female in schools is beginning to worry educators who are now even compelled to raise the question that perhaps the schools are responsible for this, not just the reckless, naughty boys." The problem has only worsened, since that interview.

Finally, it is reasonable to argue that the most significant challenge to the healthy development of a boy's brain is the effect of family stress on it. New research using functional magnetic resonance imaging (fMRI) has shown that elevated levels of stress hormones negatively affect the learning centers of a child's brain. In the summer 2015 issue of *Child Development*, the article "Tracing Differential Pathways of Risk: Associations Among Family Adversity, Cortisol, and Cognitive Functioning in Childhood" describes these effects. Primary author Jennifer H. Suor notes, "Exposure to greater levels of family instability…predicted elevated and low cortisol patterns, which were associated with lower child cognitive functioning at age 4."

It is hard to imagine something more stressful to a young boy or girl than the experience of a broken family, especially when the responsible party for the break is one or both parents. Worse, still, is the belief held by many children that he or she has contributed to that heartbreak. I'd therefore like to believe that parents, given graphic images of this research and understanding its dreadful ramifications, would experience a sel*fless* epiphany about the interests of our children rather than our own sel*fish* desires.

Zero Tolerance

While it may be true that boys are not made of "sugar and spice and everything nice," the new "zero tolerance" rules suggest a view of the young male sex as inherently bad, as the following examples attest:

- The Delaware first grader, suspended for 45 days and sentenced to reform school, all for bringing a new Cub Scout camping tool that included a small knife into school.
- The five-year-old Maryland kindergartner, suspended for showing his plastic cap gun to his friend while on the bus and then wetting his pants during the two-hour interrogation by officials prior to his parents being notified.
- The Michigan third grader who had his homemade cupcakes seized by officials because they were decorated with little plastic soldiers.

These are just a few examples of how America's idea of boyhood has changed, and we are not the better for it. The normal rough and tumble behavior of a boy's imaginative games are being criminalized or medicalized if school officials decide Johnny is misbehaving or has a "problem" that requires "treatment."

During my elementary school years, the only time I ever saw a police officer was when he helped us cross the street or coached the basketball team—and there was no counseling staff, let alone a psychologist, because we generally received "therapy" from our *married* parents in the form of discipline. During this time, any boy who did *not* play army, cops and robbers, or cowboys and Indians, using all the armaments of his creative mind, found himself either in the great minority or alone. If these policies had been in effect during my childhood, then most elementary schools would have been single sex because virtually all the boys would have been expelled—or in reform school.

Teacher: Then and Now

Although it is likely the word "teacher" brings to mind educators at school, a more accurate response would be "mother" and "father" because parents should be the primary teachers of their children. "Since parents have given children their life," asserted Pope Pius XI in his encyclical *Divini Illius Magistri* (*Those Divine Teachers*), "they are bound by the most serious obligation to educate their offspring and therefore must be recognized as the primary and principal educators." This letter should be clear to anyone—perhaps even atheists—that it is within the family where our sons (and daughters) should have instilled in them the foundation of moral and intellectual virtues as well as the joy for learning, all resulting in the self-worth and dignity our founders—both religious and political—believed to be "self-evident."

Thus, religious institutions, communities, and schools should ally to support the parents' effort. Traditionally, these were the venues of social order where boys learned the great lessons of life, particularly about truth, beauty and goodness (the "Three Transcendentals" of God) and how to live and manifest those lessons in relation to others rather than a self-centered life. The school system's role in this effort was defined as *in loco parentis*, a legal doctrine that gave educators the responsibility to act in place of the parents to provide practical *and* moral instruction. But by the mid-1900s, the public school system de-emphasized the moral in favor of the practical.

Whether in reality or the aspirations of one's mind, "the job of an educator," said Joseph Campbell, "is to teach students to see vitality in themselves," after which, I would hope, he would want those teachers to reinforce or instill the love for learning and, ultimately, the ability to learn the lessons. If one agrees with Campbell, then it is right to ask how teachers should do that. A common way over the last few decades has been to esteem students, with the well-intended hope of building their confidence; but this esteeming has often occurred without the truth of good performance as its cause.

It makes sense to question if the basis for the esteem is achievement, the hope for it, or to make children feel better about themselves. This seems to have been one side effect of the individualistic, child-centered educational model, which replaced the Classical and rote education models. Yet very often self-esteem is confused with self-*worth*, which is our intrinsic value that begins at conception and which encompasses body and soul—the essence of our being—as a gift from our Creator. Children should be trained to know this, since it is the taproot of their identity.

Self-esteem should be an outgrowth from the knowledge of that inborn self-worth, after having demonstrated Aristotle's moral excellence. Unfortunately, too many of us base our worth upon how we think others perceive us, and upon how we think of ourselves in relation to a specific event—such as a good exam grade. Children from broken homes need help understanding their intrinsic worth, and dedicated teachers, coaches and mentors can do just that. But they would be wrong to assume every student is psychologically fragile, struggling with their sense of worth such that they need to be constantly esteemed for just being, rather than for becoming, say, virtuous from success in various areas of life.

Aristotle knew our character could be moral and virtuous only if we were able to repeatedly demonstrate behaviors consonant with this description and accompanied by excellent reasoning—aka the intellectual virtue. He said, "Anything that we have to learn to do, we learn by the actual doing of it...we become just by doing just acts, temperate by doing temperate ones, brave by doing brave ones." And achievement via demonstrated behavior should be the gold standard for any esteem given in both academics and, for that matter, life.

If teachers esteem their students, wishing to encourage them to achieve, then that is hope—but not one grounded in reality. This way could be beneficial for discouraged students, but before too long it must result in a measureable success in order for it to be truthful. For many years that truth has not been realized, but esteem has continued nonetheless. An example of this illusory process is found in the discouraging results of the National Assessment of Adult Literacy. Writing in his book *Fail U*, Charles J. Sykes notes that over a two-decade period "most college graduates fell below proficiency in verbal and quantitative literacy." This perpetuates the illusion that allows students to believe they understand truth when, in reality, they are like the prisoners in Plato's "Allegory of the Cave."

In the parable, men have been shackled from birth so they are only able to look at the cave wall in front of them. Immediately behind and above them is an elevated walkway, and behind that is a fire. On that walkway are animals, people and other things from the outside world. The light from the fire helps create shadows of the things on the walkway onto the wall in front of the prisoners. Since the prisoners have only ever seen shadows, they therefore believe those are reality and truth. If one of the prisoners were to "correctly" guess which shadow would next appear, the others would affirm his wisdom. Then one day a prisoner escapes, and upon leaving the cave and experiencing the world he is shocked by the light and glare from the sun. Initially the light pains him; but eventually he realizes how it illuminates the world around him, and then understands just how little knowledge he has about reality and truth. He therefore goes on to question, explore and learn in order to know "truth." Finally, he returns to the cave to inform the others, but they reject his message and threaten him against any of his offers to free them.

This allegory teaches us many lessons. We learn that we should not become shackled by reliance on only our limited sense experience, nor deceived into thinking we have knowledge and wisdom. It also teaches us to not be inordinately influenced by those with a presumed authority, who assert that experience to be the truth. Further, the escaped prisoner represents the seeker of knowledge, wisdom and truth, the source of those being the sun that illuminates. Finally, the hostile reaction by the remaining cave dwellers represents fear of learning that the extremely limited worldview is not the "truth," making a different view seem threatening.

I want to be fair to today's public school teachers. They face difficulties unknown to Socrates, Plato, and Aristotle, or educators during the Enlightenment: classrooms with many ill-equipped and ill-behaved students whom they are compelled to teach; interfering or uncaring parents; and lawyers. Today a teacher's biggest challenge comes from students whose families—many of whom are broken and without a father—have poorly formed their children's character and impaired their learning and discipline. Conversely, a boy's biggest challenge can be the curriculum, or the teacher's sex, personality and overarching philosophy; these make it right for parents to examine and, if necessary, seek redress via a parochial, private or charter school. This is particularly important when foreign competitors outperform our students in science and math, while ours excel in the "new science" that teaches knowledge and truth are relative and boys can become girls despite the truth of their XY chromosomes.

As families deteriorate, so does the parental involvement, making any redress or proper formation of our boys unlikely at best—and *no* amount of financial aid to schools will correct this. Achievement is, therefore, too often unrealized because educators have the more difficult task of finding and developing the vitality described by Joseph Campbell. Teaching to the slowest or to the brightest in the same class is difficult, if not impossible. This can therefore make it easier and understandable to esteem a boy for, say, effort, despite getting a poor grade—and we're back in Plato's cave of illusion.

In my elementary school, the grading scale was E for excellent, G for good, F for fair, and U for unsuccessful. For some, that "E" only represented "effort." Today it is easier to reward when the grades are curved and promotions are social. However, we cannot have bridges, airplanes, or software built by adults who, while in school, were esteemed despite being suboptimal students, or else we will give companies additional reasons to lobby for more H1B visas from Asia. That E for effort is not helpful to either the boy or society.

Teacher Gender

In "The Why Chromosome: How a Teacher's Gender Affects Boys and Girls," published in 2006 in the journal, *Education Next*, professor Thomas S. Dee of Swarthmore College analyzed academic performance of approximately 25,000 eighth graders. In this study he assessed the effect a teachers' sex had on how they perceived the students' performance, and how the students engaged with the subject when taught by teachers of the same or opposite sex as the sex of the students. The results helped him draw one main conclusion: "Regardless of the academic subject, boys are two to three times more likely than girls to be seen as disruptive, inattentive, and unlikely to complete their homework" when taught by women than when taught by men. In this study sample, the percentage of female teachers for math, science, reading and history ranged from more than half to upwards of 92%. That influence matters. "Simply put," Dee asserts, "girls have better educational outcomes when taught by women and boys are better off when taught by men."

This adverse gender effect on boys is significant, because it can label them negatively in their own eyes and those of subsequent teachers, with repercussions throughout their academic career—brief though that may prove to be. And since females make up the vast majority of primary and secondary school teachers, additional concerns would be reasonable. The ramifications of the findings in this study indicate that boys may miss out on opportunities for educational advancement throughout high school, including scholarships, which then affects their access to colleges that depend upon qualified students for their enrollment. The chokehold of political correctness prevents us from exploring the truth of this problem, and therefore its solution. How different from the academies of the past.

The Academy That Was

The history of Western Civilization, from antiquity to the middle of the twentieth century, gives evidence to the importance of forming boys into virtuous men. This understanding developed and progressed because of accomplished mentors. Of the Greek schools, Sparta formed patriotic soldiers while Athens strove for the fully formed and refined man. "We cultivate," wrote Pericles, Athenian statesman and general, "the mind without the loss of manliness."

The Academy had as its origin the ancient Greek mythological hero, Academos, because of the wisdom he demonstrated in preventing the destruction of Athens. In these schools, Greek boys were diligently trained in athletics and health; as they matured, the program added training in academics, ethics, and morality, culminating in visits by philosophers for lectures, debates and discussions. That Plato and Aristotle would each select a school to which each would attach his name and reputation gives a clear indication of the importance and value of these programs.

Plato was a student of perhaps the most important of teachers, Socrates, and learned from his master the back-and-forth inquiry famously known as the "Socratic Method." These exchanges were not circular in nature but rather spiral, because they moved the student toward a deeper understanding of the subject. Plato's motivation was to allow students the opportunity to use reasoning and intellect in pursuit of the truth of the realities surrounding them, including their meaning and purpose—however uncomfortable—thereby expanding their knowledge and leading to wisdom.

Aristotle details his understanding of "happiness" in his *Nicomachean Ethics*. As human beings develop, he asserted that happiness becomes a human being's ultimate goal. Today's culture, however, misunderstands happiness as that fleeting but desperately sought-after feeling, one that is dependent upon the external. More accurately, its emphasis is on what others can do for us, producing the multiple self-centered "me" generations. The Greek master meant something entirely different.

When communicating happiness, the ancient world meant *eudaimonia* (good spirit, human flourishing), a trait in which one's virtuous character, developed in accordance with good reason, is *given* to others rather than that temporary state of good emotion *received* from others or other things. Aristotle asserted that childhood behavioral training in virtuous living would form habits from repeatedly "doing good," and would ultimately result in one "becoming good."

Aristotle believed we should strive for excellence in anything we do, make reasoned and wise choices in all aspects of our lives, and learn to couple that excellence with virtuous or moral character for the *benefit of the community*. So, for Aristotle, "It is the characteristic of a magnanimous man to ask no favor, but to be ready to do kindness to others." Recognizing our ability to reason is uniquely human, and excellence in our reasoning reflects part of our virtue. Therefore, for Aristotle, "Virtue is the perfection of reason," making a nation's primary purpose the education of its citizens to become enlightened *and* virtuous. So while he taught "educated men are as much superior to uneducated men as the living are to the dead," he also anticipated the teaching of Jesus by noting "we should behave to our friends as we would have our friends behave to us." Of course, Jesus included all classes of people, including enemies, something that could not be said of the Greek master.

In contrast with the narcissism of today, the above model valued consideration of others while striving for excellence, not only for one's own benefit but also for the social order. Training in the Classical Academy involved both reason and morality, and from that education, a boy's self-esteem resulted from an awareness of his inherent dignity, powers of reason, and proven ability to live as he was designed—which included a fully functioning intellect and morality in order to find meaning in life and fulfill his purpose for existence. Self-esteem did not result from poor reasoning despite good effort, nor from a bumper sticker or the self-proclaimed greatness of a selfie. Children should be taught this throughout their formative years, as it has historically been the basis of the Christian model of education.

The Hebrew Scriptures of the Bible tell us the prophet Daniel made clear the value of such teaching, "They that are learned shall shine as the brightness of the firmament: and they that instruct many to justice, are as stars for all eternity." Rabbi Jonathan Sacks attributes Jewish intellectual prowess to the decision to "worship an invisible God," thereby prioritizing the reasoning mind over the primitive senses. To that end, centers of formal Jewish scholarship, "yeshivas," emerged after the end of the Roman Empire.

Literate Christianity built upon its Jewish brethren to an educational renaissance, out of which developed a formalized basic education of the "liberal arts" that emphasized reason and virtue as well as the concepts of liberty, science, art and the sanctity of human rights and life. This educated faith preserved from destruction ancient texts containing the wisdom of Aristotle, Cicero and Virgil, and then spread that wisdom throughout Europe.

Included in this education was the emphasis that all had dignity, and the mind and conscience could be fully formed for the glory of God and the good of one's fellow man. This ultimately developed into perhaps the greatest collaboration of church and state: the university system. From this, Christian scholars such as Thomas Aquinas and Bonaventure broadened the study of Greco-Roman philosophy to inform theology and subsequent church doctrine, each based upon intellect, will and inspired faith. Together they refined the understanding of truth, goodness and beauty, and how they tie in with the three theological virtues of faith, hope and love. Thomas More was a product of this education, resulting in him being described as "a man of singular virtue."

As secularization took hold, schools eventually pulled away from their religious roots. During a recent visit to Columbia University, I stood in the quad facing the historic Low Memorial Library. Looking up, I saw its inscription, "For the advancement of the public good and the glory of Almighty

God," and wondered how many—or how few—of the students, faculty, and administration were conscious of this message, let alone sought to fulfill it. I was surprised it hadn't been defaced as "hate speech."

In forming the American educational experiment, founders such as John Adams, Thomas Jefferson, James Madison, and Benjamin Franklin were significantly influenced by the Classical governance philosophies of the ancient traditions of the Greeks, Romans, Hebrews and Christians, recognizing the significance of building a reasoned and virtuous citizenry. Franklin, echoing Cicero and Augustine, believed this type of education should not only help students develop their intellect but also their sense of "right and wrong," and be able "to govern his Passions." Jefferson echoed this sentiment by saying, "The objects of primary education, which determine its character and limits, are to improve his morals." Influenced as they undoubtedly were by the Christian Gospels, their hope was that the virtue in those books, coupled with the reason of the philosophers, would help form this new republic—and prevent a collapse similar to that suffered by those ancient governments in Greece and Rome. Jefferson, thinking about the nation's future descendants, was more spiritual than formally religious, and asserted, "the principal foundations of future order will be laid here" and "the first elements of morality, too, may be instilled into the minds [of our children]."

These intellectual masters believed a rigorous education of both reason and moral character was based upon universal truths and natural law embedded by our Creator into our hearts at birth. However, if one lives as if one has his own truth and his own law, then there can be no application of reason because there is no agreement on a shared starting point; no agreement on the meaning of words; and no common, underlying and objective standard for what should comprise the common good.

The freedom sought by the Declaration of Independence was from tyranny and oppression, to allow people to flourish in their pursuit of a fulfilled life according to reason and a common standard of *truth*. Judging by the changes in education, perhaps a re-emphasis of our Declaration is needed.

The New Academy

As Kevin was nearing the beginning of his formal education, I knew that meant he would be spending less time in his informal training at home. Recalling my own primary school experience, and the benefits of its academic and moral training, I wanted something similar for him and Maureen. So by the time my son was ready for school, I was eager to gradually introduce some of the Classical tradition and prepare him for the inevitable challenges he would experience, having seen the difference when I entered the modern academy of public high school that was so different from my elementary experience.

By 1970, my freshman year, public education had already moved far away from remnants of the Classical traditions of scholarship and moral character development and toward a "comprehensive" but morally relativistic curriculum. In this program, students were empowered to choose from a vast smorgasbord of non-academic (read, "easier") "lifestyle" courses, subjects that have contributed to the slide into academic and post-academic mediocrity and moral decay. As the self-esteem movement unfolded, schools ceded to immature students, increasing freedom to make "right" and "wrong" relative to *their* definition, one that did not include traditional virtues.

As this change has advanced, the intellectual and moral formation of our students seems to have not. Our high schools and colleges have been churning out many tolerant and esteemed students, whose cheapened diplomas portend a future fraught with uncertainty—except for the debt that diploma demanded. And what of those who dropped out of college? According to the National Center for the Analysis of Longitudinal Data in Education Research (CALDER), "Over 40% of full-time students at four-year colleges fail to earn a bachelor's degree within six years, and many never complete their education." This is echoed by data from the Organization for Economic Cooperation and Development (OECD), showing that when compared with seventeen other countries, the United States comes in last. The grading system also contributed to this. Both organizations, along with many others, point to one significant reason: the students are not prepared! This is despite the vast amount of money poured into American schools.

In "Where A Is Ordinary: The Evolution of American College and University Grading, 1940–2009" by Rojstaczer and Healy, research on more than 200 schools involving more than a million students showed that the frequency of students receiving an "A" had increased almost 30% since 1960. This doesn't seem to correlate well with the performance of American students on the standardized PISA (Program for International Student Assessment) test. The researchers concluded: "As a result of instructors gradually *lowering their standards* [emphasis added], "A" has become the most common grade on American college campuses. Without regulation or at least strong grading guidelines, grades at American institutions of higher learning likely will continue to have less and less meaning." The last update of this research by Rojstaczer and Healy was completed in March 2016, and shows that grade inflation problems persist.

In this context, the dropout rates in both 2-year and 4-year colleges should make us look for an even deeper problem in our high schools; and one can be identified in the results of the American College Testing (ACT) scores that indicate whether or not students met the college readiness standard in English, reading, science and math. According to the 2016 report, scores for high school graduates *fell* from the previous year, from 28% to 26%; and those meeting none of the standards *increased* to 34% from 31% in 2015. In the PISA test results for 2015, the United States did not finish in the top *twenty* in math, reading and science. Besides the obvious concern about our competitive position in the world, one has to wonder at these results, considering the vast sums of tax dollars that have been spent on our public schools.

"I" Is Better than "A"...

A school's effort to establish self-esteem in students is probably well intentioned, and either precedes or follows similar actions by many of today's parents. But the intent has helped to create a society of individuals with an increased sense of self-importance. In "How Well Are American Students Learning," published in the Brookings Institution's *Brown Center Report on American Education,* researcher Tom Loveless writes how American educators value student happiness and self-esteem as much as academic performance, but American students' performance falls far short of students in many countries that do not emphasize self-esteem. In the section "The Happiness Factor in Student Learning," Loveless writes, "The evidence does suggest, however, that the American infatuation with the happiness factor in education may be misplaced." And this happiness is not the *eudaimonia* of human flourishing described earlier.

This infatuation comes at a steep price in terms of both dollars spent and unsatisfactory results—particularly for boys. Assessing the latest data, from 2013, the National Center for Education Statistics (NCES) reports that the United States spends 28% per student on elementary and secondary education than the average spent by member countries in the Organization for Economic Co-operation and Development (OECD). And despite this expenditure, NCES data reports that boys still underperform when compared with girls, thereby helping to highlight the relative decline in males' attendance at, and graduation from, college when compared with females. We should see this ratio as indicative of both girls' success *and* boys' failure. Education isn't a zero-sum game. Finally, according to the 2015 National Assessment of Educational Progress (NAEP), known as the "Nation's Report Card," American twelfth graders' performance in reading and mathematics declined from 2013, the prior test year. No matter which acronym you choose, the test results are not encouraging.

If we reward and esteem children for only participating, or for simply being promoted to second grade, and then extol this "excellence" by adorning the family car with bumper stickers, then we should not be surprised when we learn that these students believe it doesn't take much in order to be rewarded. The "I" of "me" becomes more important than the "A" of *proven* excellence…

…And Better than "We"

The accolades given to our children over the past several decades by well-meaning parents and educators have had a variety of side effects. Measures of empathy in college students show a decline of 40% in just the past ten years, according to a study of more than 14,000 students by the University of Michigan. According to psychologists Jean Twenge and Keith Campbell, coauthors of *The Narcissism Epidemic: Living in the Age of Entitlement*, "Our students might not be the brightest...but Americans do just fine on narcissism tests." Children must learn that others matter.

Dr. Peter Gray, of Boston College, believes this loss of empathy may in fact be due to this continuous stream of praise by adults: "They may to some degree have grown up believing what they were told. To the degree that they did, they would become narcissists, because the things they were told are exactly the kinds of things that narcissists believe about themselves." He also believes it is the increased competition for better grades that drives this "looking out for number one" mentality. But this is an unhealthy form of competition, absent of virtue, and not the kind that should be encouraged in the primary grades. The esteeming has led to self-absorption and entitlement philosophy, all of which contribute to the "snowflake" tantrums of students and, increasingly, college professors.

Knowing Kevin and Maureen are, like me, not close to being perfect, narcissistic personality disorder was one diagnosis I knew neither of them would ever have. My hope was that each would know their inherent worth and dignity as human beings with the proper blend of encouragement, love, and discipline, and be esteemed only for having become true and virtuous achievers.

In Kevin's early years, I became more aware of the intrusion of political correctness into the culture, particularly in our schools. Truth, based upon an observable, measurable reality that we used to discover by reasoned exploration of ideas, was increasingly being hijacked to satisfy the new culture's subjective desires and feelings. This culture consisted of educators and administrators formed during the social and post-modern upheaval of the 1960s and 1970s, and have since caved in to the new radicals and their imagined grievances.

CHAPTER 10

Political Correctness: The New B.S. Degree

*If the freedom of speech is taken away, then dumb and
silent we may be led, like sheep to the slaughter.*

—GEORGE WASHINGTON

*If a nation expects to be ignorant and free…
it expects what never was and never will be.*

—THOMAS JEFFERSON

IF U.S. HISTORY IS STILL being taught in the new academy, then the course must be bypassing the first amendment of the Constitution that "prohibits the making of any law…abridging the freedom of speech." Ignorance of this subject is the fertile ground from which grows the new speech and behavior codes of trigger warnings and safe spaces, all of which curb free speech in our schools. These factors coincided with test results showing how poorly high school students have performed during assessments of proficiency in U.S. history, as indicated by the 2014 National Assessment of Educational Progress (NAEP). But poor test results are only one problem.

Let's be clear about whose freedoms are being trampled. Students (and the rare professor) expressing themselves on subject matter that does *not* align with the progressive philosophy, find their speech curtailed, penalized and/

or banished outright. Those holding to progressivism, however, have total freedom. Thanks to the liberty upon which this Republic was founded, Progressives and Conservatives each have the right to exercise their respective philosophy; but our Founders would never have countenanced a right for schools to teach only one of them.

The free expression and exchange of ideas, once a hallmark of the Academy, is a thing of the past in many schools and in increasing areas of society. Many who demand tolerance and, ultimately, acceptance of their position are themselves completely intolerant of and hostile to both the opposing ideas and to the person expressing those ideas—no matter how reasoned that opposition is. We now see the same behavior in our politics. Contrary viewpoints are frequently interpreted as bigoted and hateful, when nothing could be further from the truth. The weak reasoning demonstrated by those making this interpretation make them unable and unwilling to engage in that spiraling Socratic dialogue. Perhaps their emotional response is because they, like the prisoners in Plato's cave, fear the light of truth. The educational system is their cave, and the grievances instilled in them are the shackles that maintain their ignorance. The result of this fear is curtailed freedoms, manifested by speech codes, trigger warnings and the guarded communication that stems from them, particularly those pertaining to race, faith, sex, and gender.

The purpose of this branding is to delegitimize, marginalize, and perhaps criminalize the subject and person. The ultimate goal is to silence. We have seen evidence of this in recent years at several top-tier colleges and universities, including Catholic schools that have punished Catholic professors for defending *Catholic* teaching. Thus we've lost some of the traditional protections fought for by our founders. No more can one express an honestly held opinion—let alone an evidenced-based *fact*—particularly when "facts" are forced from the realm of objective reality to the dominion of subjective imagination.

Schools, particularly colleges, have enshrined speech codes for the students they have thoroughly esteemed, efforts designed to protect them from words and ideas that historically challenged students into becoming mature and wise adults. This maturity and wisdom resulted only after students learned both sides of an idea or issue, and then defended their position with reason while controlling their passions. Had he been teaching in a modern university, with its Post-Modern motto of "Relativism, Subjectivism, Progressivism," Saint Thomas Aquinas would have been ridden out on a rail for proposing objective, natural and absolute truths. Our overpriced colleges have weak administrations that have become in "loco *permissive* parentis" for their hypersensitive students, affirming the students' intolerance after quaking at their tantrums. They have taught the children that their unruly and violent outbursts, not their academics, will, in fact, succeed—at least in school. My experience was different.

In elementary school I learned to not litter or pollute, largely because harmful effects had been objectively verified as truth. By the time Kevin's generation arrived, schools were teaching about the inherent immorality of capitalism (especially the American kind), and its engine being the source of global warming that was destroying our planet. (Or was it an impending ice age? For now, it is "climate change," a reality that has presumably occurred since far longer than we've been around.) And while it is, of course, right to explore the evidence of the issues and the attendant opinions, the drive to convict the evil West of its purported climate crimes without such evidence, and then sentence it to trillions of dollars to correct, is dishonest at best. Although it is right to investigate the bad aspects of capitalism, an honest exploration would compel one to acknowledge the enormous good that resulted from that economic system.

In elementary school I learned that "in 1492 Columbus sailed the ocean blue," and that he was one of history's great men who risked everything in order to explore the world and open its riches to all. I did not hear anything about the bad side effects of this exploration, and I should have. But by the time Kevin was in grammar school, Columbus had been turned into a "greedy white European genocidal war criminal" responsible for decimating the "noble" Indian tribes, despite the evidence that the pre-Columbian health of indigenous peoples had been broadly in decline and that the vast majority of deaths were from disease transmission. The latter is a tragic but unintended consequence of ongoing population shifts and historic exploration. And rarely have American students heard of the atrocities committed by various tribal nations against each other and which they *initiated* against the Europeans.

In contrast, during the recent Ebola epidemic, more than 10,000 Africans died within a single year. Several cases were diagnosed on other continents, the result of people traveling from Africa. But had the economic system of the West been anything other than capitalism, with its financial incentives to develop the modern medical system, the spread of that horrible disease by innocent travelers could have resulted in a scenario similar to that involving European exploration of the Americas. Yet Kevin's generation would have heard nothing about those travelers being called "murderers."

In elementary school I learned that intentionally doing wrong was immoral and a sin against God and nature, and therefore required repentance, discipline, transformation, and reconciliation in order to restore right order and our loving relationship—ideally with both God and the offended person. But by the time Kevin was in school, America was hearing no references to "sin" and few of "God," "personal responsibility," and "morality." Instead, we heard, "society's fault," "mistake," and "emotional problems"—OR, the post-modernist's creed that *wrong* can no longer be asserted because morality is, after all, relative to each person's definition of it.

The examples above could rightly be debated in our schools, and they should be. Unfortunately, it is highly unlikely a debate would occur because of the looming threat by "the language police" described by educator Diane Ravitch in her book of that title. Thus, for too many years, students have had no opportunity to engage in edifying debates because political correctness does not allow it. The objectors close their ears, stamp their feet and shout down their opponents—or prevent those with differing positions from even entering the debate. The emphasis has moved away from traditional virtues of Prudence, Justice, Fortitude and Temperance toward the new "virtues" of Tolerance, but only of the radical left's philosophy; Diversity, but not in opinions about that philosophy; Inclusion, but only of those who agree with that philosophy; and Sustainability, but only of the endurance of that world view. As with "truth," virtues related to personal morality have been replaced so that each person can decide his or her morality—and truth—all at the expense of lagging scholarship, civil discourse and E Pluribus Unum. Today's academy is the epicenter of the evils known as moral relativism, subjectivist victimhood and character assassination, philosophies that are incompatible with Plato's single, overarching *Good* as the highest *Truth* and Aristotle's *Nous*, or *Primary Intelligence*. But were they and Socrates teaching in our decaying academies, their only hope would lie in America's free enterprise system, and the opportunity to form their own university. Otherwise, there might be a fight over the hemlock.

At the same time my son was working his way through college, President Obama was working his way through his first term; and in that time my son would learn that philosophical criticisms of the President's *policies* could easily be branded as racism, despite the critic having animus to neither the president's race nor anyone of African ancestry.

Kevin would also learn that anyone expressing a reasoned opposition to coed military combat units, support for women choosing to remain at home with their young children rather than being at work (or at war), or questioning the assertion by some that 20% of all female college students have suffered sexual assault would very likely result in that person being branded a sexist, misogynist and, of course, a hater.

Finally, Kevin would learn that those publicly supporting traditional marriage, opposing same-sex marriage or supporting religious exemption from having to play any part related to same-sex marriage would be hounded via social media and the courts in an effort to force them into behaving in a way that would violate their deeply held beliefs and reason. Those individuals would also be labeled "homophobic," despite having neither fear nor hatred of someone with homosexuality as part of his or her nature. *The pseudointellectual mask can be held only until reasoned truth removes it—but at a cost.*

In an effort to take some measure of this outrageous abridgement of the First Amendment, Heterodox Academy developed a survey model aimed at determining which college students are afraid (or not) to speak about which subjects, and why they are afraid. In one survey, completed through YourMorals.org, Heterodox used their "Fearless Speech Index" (FSI) to measure responses from several hundred students of both sexes, representing a variety of universities, about subjects such as race, gender and politics. The potential consequences identified by the students included:

1. Criticism by their professors or classmates;
2. Criticism posted on social media;
3. Having a complaint filed against them for having views that violated the schools' harassment policy or code of conduct; and
4. Being graded lower by the professor, or having the professor say that the views of the student were wrong.

The survey led to the conclusion that students identifying as "conservative" reported being much more averse to speaking about each of the three topics, and fearful about each of the named consequences.

Kevin would need to know the new rules regarding acceptable speech because violating them would likely cause him great trouble. As long as he knew the rules, he could then make a more informed choice between speaking freely—or guardedly.

But how unfortunate for Kevin, and for all of us, because the academy and its educators are supposed to model Socrates, whose virtue of humility made him always the seeker of greater knowledge. Students should be guided into a deep exploration of life's big questions in search of even bigger answers, and to be intrepid like the great philosophers and explorers throughout human history, so as to prepare young minds for a fuller life in the real world. Our academies have increasingly emphasized specific skill sets, particularly in the technical and scientific fields. "But," writes Allan Bloom, in *The Closing of the American Mind*, "a great university presented another kind of atmosphere, announcing that there are *questions that ought to be addressed by everyone* but are not asked in ordinary life…" (emphasis added).

Instead, educators and their pusillanimous administrators have contrived the "victim" status in their students, and the subsequent entitlements. This identity can be forever used with (self-) righteous indignation by its victims against their imagined oppressors—in some cases those very same educators. By doing this, neither administrators, educators nor students will understand (at least not yet) the sad irony that this unearned status will forever label those students—to the world and, eventually, to themselves—as "the undeserving."

The Progressive March to Regression

I believe most teachers and administrators may be well intentioned, but the predominant progressive philosophy behind those intentions makes them the pavement on our children's road to academic mediocrity and societal decline. This system affirms the supremacy of radical individual freedom and its associated coursework, which is funded and enforced by big government—with our tax dollars.

In a 2005 *Washington Post* article entitled "College Faculties: A Most Liberal Lot," Howard Kurtz describes how surveys of full-time professors at 183 colleges reveal that 72% are liberal, and in the top-tier universities it is 87%. In its 2010–2011 faculty survey, UCLA's Higher Education Research Institute (HERI) reported that the great majority (68%) of professors were liberal or far left, and of those two groups, the highest percentage were females.

"Progressives rule higher education," asserts the opening sentence in *Passing on the Right: Conservative Professors in the Progressive University*. Authors Jon A. Shields and Joshua M. Dunn note the disproportionate progressive presence in the ranks of college professors, as surveys reveal under 10% of those in the social sciences and humanities fields are Republican (*not* identifying as conservative), and one-quarter in the social science are Marxist (let alone, simply Liberal).

It should come as no surprise to know that the movement away from the *rational* Liberal education in the Classical Tradition and toward the *emotive* progressive liberal education comes at the expense of Western Civilization—the greatest ever and the foundation of both our culture and the very university in which those teachers work. In "Making Citizens: How American Universities Teach Civics," The National Association of Scholars (NAS) documents the great decline in traditional education of American exceptionalism, and the civic responsibilities associated with it. The comprehensive report notes, "In consequence, American students' knowledge about their institutions of self-government has collapsed. According to the Association of American Colleges & Universities' report *A Crucible Moment: College Learning & Democracy's Future* (2012), 'Only 24% of graduating high school seniors scored at the proficient or advanced level in civics in 2010, fewer than in 2006 or in 1998,' 'Half of the states no longer require civics education for high school graduation,' and 'Among 14,000 college seniors surveyed in 2006 and 2007, the average score on a civic literacy exam was just over 50 percent, an 'F'.'" Could this be due to the way educators see America's history? For many, we are racist, despite making tremendous efforts to eliminate that scourge, or we are militaristic, despite giving incalculable treasure to defeat, for example, the twin plagues of fascism and communism.

Replacing our heritage and the civic duty it inspired, with the "New Civics of progressive political activism" described by the NAS, is both tragic and shameful. Our academy should help students engage in a full examination and understanding of "Western Civ" while also learning about other civilizations and cultures. This would be helpful as our nation's demographics continue to change due to an immigration policy that has allowed greater access for people from nations having little or no experience with that tradition. However, they probably won't learn it as many earlier generations of Americans before them had, and this may widen the separations of our fault lines.

Following in the anarchic footsteps of their professors and administrators, themselves formed in the campus tumult during the 1960s, today's protesters increasingly foment discord and violence against an imagined "oppressive Western patriarchy or hegemony." But in doing so, they fail to see the great flaw in their thinking and their actions: *the freedom to act this way is a by-product of that very same civilization.* Among this group are recent illegal or undocumented immigrants, some who left their homeland due to tyranny of one sort or another. They, too, fail to understand that their uncontrollable passions cause a real oppression, one that will come back to bite them when their adopted country becomes less free due to that very same oppression.

In the play, "A Man for All Seasons," Will Roper scolds Thomas More for not having Richard Rich arrested, despite no law having been broken. More, the product of a Classical Liberal education, defends the tradition, logic and importance of English law, saying he would give even the Devil the benefit of those laws. Outraged, Roper blusters that he would cut down all the laws to get at the Devil, to which More forcefully responds, "And when the last law was down, and the Devil turned on you…where would you hide…do you really think you could stand upright in the winds that would blow then?" This is what is happening as laws and traditions of "Western Civ" are eliminated from our campuses.

There is a further irony in all this: the pathetic administrations subject to mayhem from the anti-Western protests are largely responsible for the problem. They have been hoisted on their own petard, a wonderful phrase whose meaning would escape virtually all of their students, since the dead, white, English male responsible for it has been expelled from school.

Ultimately, we all suffer. Ignorance of our tradition and its moral foundation will weaken all of us—including the protesters—and cause further fracturing of our nation into disparate groups. Will this unfold into a societal or, worse, national rot from within as the West continues to turn on itself by decimating its families, schools and virtue traditions, and by graduating undereducated but entitled "victims"? In *Caesar and Christ: The Story of Civilization*, historian Will Durant wrote about the fall of Rome: "A great civilization is not conquered from without until it has destroyed itself within." His words made me wonder if, in 1,500 years, an historian will describe the downfall of the United States of America as another example. Let us hope not, and work to fulfill that hope.

I wanted something different for my children. But whether public or private, I wondered if I would find it. Would Kevin's teachers be able to proclaim his intellectual and moral virtue? Maybe. But I was more concerned they would esteem him more for any "tolerant," "inclusive," and "sustainable" behavior, and not be able to justifiably proclaim how educated, responsible, and virtuous he had become. My frame of reference was a primary education completed in a traditional Catholic school, an experience that is increasingly difficult to replicate—even in Catholic schools.

Catholic Elementary Education

From the late eighteenth century, Catholics have significantly impacted American education, echoing the impact of their Protestant predecessors in the Colonial era and their medieval ancestors in Europe. But unlike any other time, this impact came mostly from women—and an extraordinary group they were. An organization of Catholic sisters moved throughout the land, following the missionary tradition of their forebears. Among their great contributions are the many thousands of schools they helped build and run. Their models included Augustine, Aquinas, and Ambrose, saints all, themselves students of Greek philosophers. Their discipline with high academic and moral standards attracted many who were not Catholic. Lacking perfection, they sometimes meted out excessive discipline and became the butt of jokes, especially from baby boomers. But most were esteemed because of the great work they did, including in orphanages and hospitals.

The Sisters of Charity ran the school I attended during the 1960s. Their influence upon me was significant. They expected much, and whatever praise was given came *after* students demonstrated the ability to meet their academic and moral standard. Boys were allowed to be boys, encouraged to be active and respectable while striving for scholarship and a well-formed conscience. We were held accountable with tough love, a couple of times justifiably very tough in the form of a large hickory ruler brought down on knuckles (perhaps that was the reason my wife struggled to slide the ring onto my finger).

Although the principal and most teachers had zero tolerance for character deficiencies, these religious women understood and encouraged the boyish behavior known since the beginning of time—including my schoolyard scuffles. Thank goodness for that. It is worth noting that the psychologist's couch was never needed, neither were pharmacist's pills. And the lawyer's number was never dialed. As the number of these consecrated women diminished, time has made clear that their imperfections are dwarfed by their great successes. In their void moved the progressive philosophy, and the self-esteem and self-centeredness that spring from it—along with zero tolerance for boyhood.

If my boyhood altercations occurred within today's policies, I would in all likelihood be suspended from school, but only after meeting with the guidance counselors, social workers, vice principal, and principal. The school's legal counsel would be on standby for the eventual lawsuit brought by one or both sets of parents. Each would challenge both the punishment and the school's authority, thereby modeling the disrespect of authority for their children to emulate. Most importantly, IF both of our parents arrived, then at least one couple would have done so via separate cars—because they would be divorced.

Thinking back to a scene in *Anne of Green Gables*, I shudder to think what would happen today if Gilbert Blythe had been caught grabbing Anne Shirley's pigtail. He would very likely be charged with sexual assault. Of course he would have countersued, having been assaulted by Anne and her slate.

Demanding Teachers Matter

I found that while Kevin was going through his school years, I would periodically recall similar experiences during mine, comparing them with his. I was glad to learn that as in my schooling, self-esteem initiatives were not employed at my son's school. When I think back to my elementary school teachers, I cannot recall one who coddled me or who sought to enhance my self-esteem. Being Christian, they did emphasize our inherent self-worth and dignity by being children of God, a God who loved us so much he wanted to become one of us. I had some vague sense that that was a good thing. In my schooling, virtually every teacher, especially the sisters and the men, had excellent "bull" detectors, and only foolish students failed to learn that lesson early on. They weren't so interested in how we felt about the questions, only in the quality of our answers and the thinking that led to them.

But as understanding as those teachers were, I recall that boys, predominantly, carried notes home to parents; were sent to the principal's office; had their ears pulled; or had to write "I must not…" on the chalkboard one hundred times. In fact, I see the face of one of those boys every time I look into the mirror. Yet in all the classes I had with male teachers, those punishments rarely happened. The male teachers had a different presence, a physicality that intimidated us—because they could in those days. There was no threat from family services, nor any worries of being opposed by a phalanx of parents and lawyers. While the large principal of Kevin's elementary school did have to consider these modern opponents, his imposing presence was such that it was unlikely a problem would reach that level. And, the parents supported him.

The inference boys in my school drew was that certain female teachers (never the religious sisters) could at least be tested, similar to a boy being more willing to test his mother than his father. The reality was simply that we would rarely test the men, because the power they exuded was intimidating. Plus, the male teachers were more tolerant of the boys moving around a bit during the class, and recognized boys' need for physical activity out in the playground. If there was trouble, it was handled with speed and soon resolved. The sisters were tolerant, just not as much as the male teachers. This was similar to Kevin's experience; there was no likelihood his principal could be tested, despite how the boys might try to outmaneuver a female teacher.

Looking back at my time, another factor was the great likelihood we would identify with our male teachers, or see our fathers in them. But today, with so many boys having no father around or no fatherly involvement, it is unlikely they would be capable of any identification with a male teacher or tolerant of any disciplinary action. And I'm having great difficulty recalling more than a couple of girls who were known to be troublemakers, and none who today would have misshapen knuckles or enlarged ears.

Parochial Power…Receding?

Having been sent to a public high school, I experienced a first when my sociology, psychology, and civics teachers asked me, in the context of a statement from a classmate or textbook, "How does that make you feel?" This was my introduction to the educational philosophy and pedagogy of post-modernism.

This method asserts that "truth" is found *not* in what the author was intending, by a careful examination of context such as his timeframe and its language, but in the relativism of each student's personal interpretation. This approach was deceptively invidious, because any strongly *felt* answer was impossible to be wrong (as mine often were in math class). But in my Catholic school, classmates and I had little interest and absolutely no feelings about each other's answers, except when someone's was so far off the mark the others could enjoy the subsequent scolding. We were either right or wrong. Gray areas were rare.

This was made clear during 7th grade geography class one warm spring afternoon, when my languid classmates were not impressing Sister Anna Marian with their acumen about South America. It seemed to be one incorrect answer after another. Suddenly she fell silent, and her cheeks became increasingly florid. The room seemed to darken, a familiar change warning of an imminent storm. She, like all the sisters, wore a full, dark blue habit and black, chunky-heeled shoes. Her bearing was intense, and her ruddy cheeks reflected that. Sister's thick glasses greatly magnified her eyes, making it difficult to not imagine you were looking at a fish through an aquarium.

The predictable storm came. When she sternly asked us for the name of the largest city in Brazil, I, alone, haltingly raised my hand and mumbled, "Sao Paolo." Her sudden turn away from me and toward the class made her habit billow, and after silently probing them with her magnified eyes she barked, "How many think he's right?" Their reaction would have made sense if we had instead been on the *Titanic* while it was going down, and I had recommended to the captain that everyone remain on the ship to finish dessert. Not one of my friends raised their hand in a show of support. "He's right!" She barked, to my everlasting smug satisfaction, and then leveled a storm blast at them that I relished—until my next wrong answer.

And it wasn't until I fathered Maureen that I appreciated Sister's other mastery of those hickory rulers—keeping twelve inches of distance between boys and girls at school dances in an effort to encourage our modesty and moral well-being.

While I didn't always appreciate it then, I eventually understood why Sister had sternly emphasized the value of diagramming sentences and memorizing the truths of our faith, so when you needed each—at any time in life—each was easily retrieved from our memories. The practice and drills made it more likely we would achieve the virtue of excellence extolled by Aristotle.

Similar situations played themselves out every day in Catholic schools around the world. Whether it was geography, history, or moral theology, the sisters weren't concerned about our sensitivities per se, but whether or not we were right, knew the material, and could present our reasoning—because the outcome was of profound importance. Our feelings about faith were important, but not at the expense of intellect and good character. We were being trained in the realities of the natural law designed by our Creator. The gray areas generally occurred after we lived in discord with that law—or got to public school.

Today, unfortunately, it is sometimes as difficult to find the "Catholic" in parochial schools as it is to find a consecrated sister, because the sweeping cultural changes have elevated the rights and study of morally relativistic ideologies over the sacred and unchanging doctrines, and educational principles, of the very church that founded and formed these schools. These changes have been advanced and celebrated by administrations and faculty that espouse a version of Catholicism—and Jesus Christ—heretofore unknown, having given in to the temptation of federal dollars and capitulated to the cultural "isms" antithetical to the faith of the Church. In a misguided effort to become more relatable to the spiritual but not religious Jesus—as a man but not God—is no greater than, say, Buddha, Mohammad or whomever one conjures. Scandal and disarray have ensued as faith has declined and the church pews emptied.

The severity of this degradation was such that it caused Pope John Paul II to issue the Apostolic Constitution, *Ex Corde Ecclesia* ("From the Heart of the Church"), asserting, among other things, that Catholic colleges and universities must keep their Catholic identity and, in large part, adhere to the teachings of the Church. According to the Cardinal Newman Society, an organization whose mission is "to promote and defend faithful Catholic education," only a small percentage of these schools meet this requirement.

So perhaps the greatest worry for Catholic parents is that their children will graduate from a Catholic college with much more debt and much less—if any—*Catholic* faith.

American universities—public, private and parochial—still rank highly when compared with their foreign competitors. Nineteen of the top twenty-five schools are American, according to the Academic Ranking of World Universities (ARWU), but the concern is that the declining performance in high school of American boys means fewer of them are contributing to the success of these universities. I can find evidence in my own family for this decline.

In late August of 1985, shortly after my father's death, I found his fifty-year-old, leather-bound high school notebook. It was a startling discovery, and helped me realize some of the basis for his insistence on accountability.

As I carefully turned the fragile pages, I was startled by both the breadth and depth of the subjects, as well as his notes. There were the occasional humorous doodles in the margins pertaining to classmates, sports, and teachers, which gave me a window into the rarely seen lighter side of my father. But by far, the more interesting feature was the volume of written notes on subjects such as philosophy, physics, and ethics as well as calculus, theology, and philology. (The fact I had to look up the definition of the last course while nearing the end of graduate school was both humbling and a bit embarrassing.) During my search I could not find even a hint of "Gender Studies," "Transracialism" and the related "isms" of misandry. It was an example of the Classical education system, and made me wish that type of education had been available in my high school. I've been working hard ever since in an effort to catch up to him.

The Father

Whenever I was sent home with notes from my teachers, the punishment I received from them and my father seemed unjust, but it still benefitted me greatly that each time this happened I was going home to an intact family. At the time I certainly did not have that thought, partly because I did not like my father's punishments, and because broken families were not part of my world. It was a truth I would realize later. And the benefits were real, as research would eventually prove. I was going home to a family headed by a man who cared enough to hold his children accountable. That, sadly, cannot be said about many boys today.

For a boy, the hurt feelings from the absence of his father often lead to anger and depression, which can manifest into bullying. These emotions make sense, according to Robert Hughes, professor in the Department of Human Development and Family Science at Ohio State University. "When fathers are absent or uninvolved, boys are more likely to be aggressive and have problems getting along with their peers and teachers." He further asserts, "These problems may lead them to spend less time in school or on their schoolwork."

According to Steven H. Kaye's "The Impact of Divorce on Children's Academic Performance" and many subsequent studies, boys and girls of divorce do significantly worse on standardized achievement testing when compared with children of intact families. However, after the subsequent five years, only boys continued to struggle with that testing and generally with academics.

While divorce is only one reason for the difficulties boys face while in school, it is arguably the most significant because it causes or aggravates other cited factors such as poverty (especially in families headed by single women), reduced parental involvement (especially the father), and emotional stress. Family breakdown places an impossible burden on educators because they cannot be both parent and teacher, nor can they ignore the other students. In addition, too many of them may be strained by their own divorce. This dilemma results in tremendous tax dollars being paid to have the government make futile attempts at the Sisyphean task of raising our children—according to *its* progressive values.

Having a conservative philosophy, I prefer government intervention mainly to fulfill the limited constitutional requirements—being parents isn't one of them. But the irresponsible and selfish behavior of many mothers and fathers who have failed in their duties creates demands—often by those very same parents—for government programs in school and well beyond. This is unfair to teachers, and to the students.

We have a moral obligation to our children, but our selfishness proves to those children that we feel little obligation toward them.

Medication: A Treatment for…Boyhood?

All too often it seems that educators have either been unaware of the significant hormonal differences between boys and girls, or have chosen to ignore the science confirming those differences. One aspect of this difference is the relatively greater time and effort needed by young boys to control their emotions and calm down after they become excited or angry. I would have loved to have been able to say to some of my elementary school teachers, "Don't blame me; blame my testosterone."

Perhaps the typical teacher is unaware that one effect of estrogen, a substance girls have in greater supply than boys, is to help one become calm more quickly after excitement. Noting this, we can legitimately question the use and overuse of medications in our boys. Dr. Gurian questions the need of medication, saying, "Over four million American boys are on Ritalin, and the United States uses 80% of the world's Ritalin. Are some boys being diagnosed with brain disorders for merely acting out their boy energy in classrooms that assign more value to sitting still and being quiet?"

Therefore, has medication been used to treat boyhood? I think too often the answer is yes. But I would ask an additional question: Has medication been increasingly used to treat the harmful effects that family strife has had on boys? Noting the research on elevated levels of cortisol and on the effects of an absent father, I would argue vigorously in the affirmative. In that context, boys are overmedicated. Many typically misinterpret that wording, as I initially did, to only mean that physicians are overprescribing and/or parents are overreacting to the normal "problems" of boys. But I now believe the absence of fathers has caused such problems that both schools *and* drugs must, by default, act in place of parental love and discipline. Data from the National Survey of Children's Health, a survey of more than sixty-five thousand children, helps to support my position. The study showed that children diagnosed with ADHD had significantly more early childhood traumas—including divorce—than children not diagnosed with that disorder.

To buttress my argument even further, I'll refer to research by MIT economist David Autor and colleagues published by the Institute for Policy Research out of Northwestern University. The team of social scientists studied more than one million children born from 1992 to 2002 and found that boys from disadvantaged homes without a father exhibit far more behavioral, cognitive, and criminal predicaments than do their sisters. Interviewed by the *New York Times*, Mr. Autor noted, "Boys particularly seem to benefit more from being in a married household…with the time, attention and income that brings." In my words: Boys need their fathers, and preferably married to their mothers.

Writing on the effects of medicating children, Carl Tishler, PhD, notes: "There are no long-term data on the effects…on child development." The potential consequences of being on medication at these young ages are too serious to be casual. It would be wonderful if research could be done comparing academic performance, disciplinary intervention, and medication use on two samplings of boys from kindergarten through high school or college, with one group having significant physical activity woven into the curriculum, the other having the usual curriculum—and in boys from intact families versus broken ones.

Data from Boys Town makes clear that the impact of family breakdown is a huge factor on boys' problems and the medication used to treat those difficulties: "Despite the lack of research about its effectiveness in youth, and evidence of adverse effects, psychotropic medication rates have drastically increased in behaviorally disordered children since the early 1990s—raising concern from medical, mental health and child experts that it may be overused."

It is legitimate to debate the issue of using psychotropic drugs in children. And that discussion should inquire whether diagnostic tools are simply better; whether educators and parents are too quick to medicate rather than deal directly with the behavior simply because the drugs are available; or whether rampant family breakdown is the main reason for the behavioral problems.

Clarifying this would be vital to more accurately target medication; reduce misidentifying boys' normal behavior; and encourage parents to first consider their children before seeking divorce.

Feminism

Women have long had a presence in American schools, and comprise nearly 80% of all public school teachers. But in the last fifty years of our vast educational-industrial complex, it has become increasingly difficult to confirm their success—certainly with boys. Two big changes in recent decades have, I believe, had a disproportionately bad effect on boys: poor or absent male role models and an educational philosophy and pedagogy influenced by progressivism and gender feminism. The first change is explored elsewhere in this book, so I'll touch on the second.

The traditional feminist movement was noble, righteous and, in fact, heroic, as it successfully struggled against blatant unfairness. This effort has proven effective at improving the lives of women, and has led to a superior position in education. Christina Hoff Sommers, author of *The War Against Boys* and proof of the movement's success, refers to this as "equity feminism." However, a militant element emerged, which Sommers refers to as "gender feminism," and one that is meant, she says, "to convince women that they are victims, that they are put upon by men in every respect." They've done a good job, much to the detriment of boys and men. Since workshops, advanced degrees, careers and business enterprises have been erected upon this radical offshoot, its end is very unlikely.

This radical "third-wave" feminism has morphed into a more pathological belief system known as "intersectionality," whose doctrine and dogma assert that systemic discrimination and oppression exist against a wide variety of victims, and brought us the "identity politics" of today. Since the purported offenses include sexism, as well as racism, ableism, classism and homo/trans/xeno-phobia, the offenders must—a priori—largely come from one group: heteronormative white males oozing hegemonic masculinity (aka white, straight, successful men). Since college is both the incubator and home of this radicalism, I thought it reasonable to search a variety of college websites for material on this subject. That search revealed each had a program aimed at stamping out "toxic masculinity," a phrase that any normal man should find offensive—and indefinable. Yet these same searches uncovered no evidence of "toxic *femininity*," probably because that gender classification and all it implies is deemed offensive to those marching in the pink hat brigade.

A boy's biology, up until fairly recently, was usually tempered and guided by the presence of men in his life, principally his father, and by significant physical activity. This held true even when female teachers began outnumbering male educators. Marriages were intact, and a boy's nature, while annoying to some, was not seen as unnatural. After all, boys will be boys. And there was certainly no assumption that boys were inherently malformed or violent, or that their nature must be neutralized and their *gender* reshaped away from the traditional masculinity of their *sex* into one that is less assertive and more sensitive—in other words, more like girls.

When you look at these programs, it is easy to see why many believe this feminist element has become too divisive, causing great acrimony between and among the sexes. It has striven to force a "sameness" of the *biologic* sexes and an imagined equality of outcome, rather than equality in both the opportunity and dignity I described earlier. This relates directly to gender formation, because these groups want to deny the obviously direct linkage between gender and biology and dissociate gender from maleness and femaleness. This is illogical and ahistorical. According to Sommers, "In the view that has prevailed in American education…boys are resented, both as the unfairly privileged sex and as obstacles on the path to gender justice for girls."

Thanks to gender feminist educators (from both sexes) and the government bureaucrats who do their bidding, Title IX enforcement expanded far beyond its intended scope. The effect has been to severely diminish boys' involvement in sports programs, perhaps the only extracurricular programs where boys still excel when compared with girls. So rather than only producing the desired effect of enhancing girls, this program proved to be another example of how boys are harmed in the process. We therefore have the situation of girls being allowed to join the boys' high school wrestling and football teams.

While attending Kevin's first wrestling tournament during his freshman year of high school, I turned to look at a particular match and was startled to see one of the wrestlers had a large lump on his head covered by a skullcap. I wondered if the poor guy had some type of medical problem. At the end of the match this combatant removed the cap, and my startle turned to shock when I saw "his" growth was none other than the hair bun of a "her."

This is an impossible situation for a boy, and bad all the way around. If the boy wins, then all he did was *beat a girl*. In all my life, I never knew an experience where it was considered a good thing to beat a girl or, worse, to beat up a girl. And if the poor boy lost, well, then he *lost to a girl*, a result that would doom him with his peers during those crucial formative years. As indicated earlier, educational leaders are hyper-focused on students' self-esteem, yet they would allow this debacle without considering its detrimental effect on the boy. This forced effort at co-ed athletics is also fraudulent, because as bodies mature, nature will eliminate the weaker females from these sports, but at a severe cost along the way to both the replaced boys and to our culture.

The boy—and in all likelihood only the boy—would be arrested had this occurred outside of a wrestling match or in his marriage. Is there a father who would allow a second of that physicality toward his daughter on a date? How could parents and educators not have realized this would further desensitize boys and girls to their differences and to girls' historic—dare I say it—femininity, adding harshness to the relationships that are increasingly being strained in our culture? Trying to equalize the genders is another exercise in social engineering, when that can never be accomplished because of our different sexes. Most importantly, what meaning does this have for the health of relationships between boys and girls that are already strained?

My sense is that most people would not like females involved with wrestling or football, or in the front lines of military combat; but if it's going to be forced upon us via lawsuits and gender activists, then I think it should at least be separate from the males, just like single-sex classrooms. In her 2013 book,

Freedom Feminism, Sommers describes a philosophy I believe would help reduce the acrimony between the sexes, which ultimately affects the family and its boys. Rather than being "at war with femininity and masculinity," or seeing the two sexes "as warring tribes," Freedom Feminism simply "affirms for women what it affirms for everyone: dignity, fairness and liberty" while noting the natural interdependence of the two sexes on each other. One cannot exist without the other!

Sexual Predators?

Boys have increasingly found themselves labeled—a priori—as sexual harassers, and subsequently punished for behavior once considered only mildly offensive or immature and which resulted in measured discipline. But while preparing for college, they and their parents must know that the enthusiastic greeting found in the acceptance letter hides the belief of many in schools and, for awhile, in the federal government, that each boy poses a risk of being a carnal marauder. This belief was made clear during "student welcome day" at a school my daughter briefly attended, by all the posters, fliers, and videos warning about the apparently rampant scourge of toxic behavior—of *only* its male students. While I knew my checkbook and daughter were welcome, I didn't sense the same about *me*.

As our culture has increasingly coarsened, it is especially right to challenge, punish and, ideally, prevent any sexual harassment or abuse perpetrated by *both* sexes. Being a father of a daughter, I am particularly angered when an *actual* offense is committed, and I know Kevin would vigorously defend Maureen were she a true victim. At the same time, it is terribly wrong to assume a male college student is guilty simply by accusation *and* by being male. But that is the reality on college campuses and increasingly in the corporate world (one that has made these young men, ironically, a *legitimate* victim group).

The new policies are a natural outgrowth of the deeply entrenched gender militancy within our colleges. But the harmful philosophy behind these guidelines became emboldened and empowered when the Obama administration broadened Title IX legislation to campus sexual assault in which "preponderance of evidence" replaced "due process," and harmed many in the process. The change was so fraught with problems that both conservative and progressive feminists were among its detractors, including Sommers, Heather MacDonald and Elizabeth Bartholet. Among their concerns is the absence of hallmark legal principles for the accused, because in the college kangaroo courts neither due process nor the presumption of innocence is welcome. Another formidable factor is the federal government's pressure on colleges to improve their campus sexual assault statistics—whether or not either that improvement or those statistics is legitimate.

A common statistic that drove this change is that 20 to 25% of female college students suffer a completed or attempted rape. This figure agrees with the Progressive Left's narrative, and so has been bandied about without much close scrutiny—until recently. Writing in *City Journal*, Dr. MacDonald explodes this data as well as the harmful falsehoods behind it. In "The Campus Rape Myth," MacDonald draws a striking contrast (the only kind possible) between the aforementioned crime wave and violent crime data in Detroit for 2006. When combining a variety of crimes per 100,000 residents, the rate was only 2.6%. "The one-in-four statistic would mean," she notes, "that every year, millions of young women graduates have suffered the most terrifying assault.... Such a crime wave would require nothing less than a state of emergency." She goes on to imagine colleges placing a ban on all male college applicants. But I know that would never happen, because colleges need the money generated by men's sports in order to fund programs that seem to target those very same athletes.

Greater attention should be paid, it would seem, to a rigorous study completed by the Bureau of Justice Statistics, showing the "assault" rate at only 6.1 per 1,000 and trending downward since the 1990s. Progressives seem to be quite liberal with their definitions of "sexual assault," perhaps unwilling to cite that which was defined by the U.S. Supreme Court in a 1999 ruling pertaining to student-on-student harassment and the harm that is asserted: "We conclude that such an action will lie only for harassment that is so severe, pervasive and objectively (i.e., *evidently*) offensive that it effectively bars the victim's access to an educational opportunity or benefit." But the criteria used by colleges are frequently subjective.

Once again, in an effort to do a good, a great evil has resulted. Gross injustices toward men have occurred, with two of the most glaring examples being the rape hoaxes involving members of the Duke University lacrosse team in 2006 and the Phi Kappa Psi fraternity at the University of Virginia six years later. The pendulum seems to have swung from insensitivity and inaction by colleges on behalf of legitimate victims to hypersensitivity and excessively punitive actions sweeping across our nation's campuses against the accused.

These actions cause deep and lasting harm, and recall Cicero's warning, "Extreme justice is extreme injustice." Although both the Duke and UVA groups were exonerated, press reports years after the conclusion of the case make me confident they have been forever scarred from the experiences. Efforts aimed at defending the increasing numbers of falsely accused and wrongly punished young men have resulted in advocacy groups such as Save Our Sons and Families Advocating for Campus Equality, in an effort to oppose the mobbing social justice warriors that have taken over our schools. The parents involved in these groups have seen their once thriving sons banished from the only pathway they've known, too many of which will be hounded by a permanent record, left to struggle with depression, post-traumatic stress disorder, hospitalization and suicide.

As with the music and media industries, the hypocrisy in college is rampant. On one hand, colleges decry the sexual violence, one that is frequently fueled by alcohol, but on the other hand, they allow that alcohol while at the same time providing free condoms. Are the latter actions contributing to the former, but resulting in more Title IX money to the schools? Can it be resolved? MacDonald's advice would be, "Don't get drunk, don't get into bed with a guy, and don't take off your clothes or allow them to be removed," as these restraints "would bring an end to the purported epidemic overnight." It is only fair to urge similar behavior on men; better yet, would be for men to choose the virtuous life, by treating women with respect and dignity. But when confronted by MacDonald's wisdom of encouraging girls to act modestly, prudently and responsibly, the Title IX administrator replied right off the anti-male script, "Because rape is never a woman's fault. I don't want to suggest that it is her fault." Considering their age range, it is probable that many administrators were among yesterday's sexually liberated students during the '60s and '70s. Now that the Trump administration has rescinded the previous administration's "Dear Colleague" letter, the legal process due *both* sexes should be a welcome change.

"Emasculating Men" The New Academic Major?
Much of the aforementioned indicates that in the New Academy, traditional masculinity is seen, prima facie, as dysfunctional and harmful. Further evidence is suggested by programs such as "Breaking out of the *Straight*jacket of Masculinity" (emphasis added) at Ithaca College, which presumes an inherently stuck and suffering sex because of the traditionally masculine roles of its associated gender; and, "Real Men Smile: The Changing Face of Masculinity," at Towson University, one seeming to assert that traditionally-defined masculinity is a falsehood built upon emotional dishonesty, and only by being emotionally honest (presumably like women?) will the *real* man come out.

A check of Ithaca's website revealed some irony in its use of "*straight-jacket*," since the program was sponsored by the college center for LGBT education. The Towson program, described in an April 2016 *New York Times* article by its teacher, Andrew Reiner, seems to exemplify the gender-bender, gender-feminist philosophy. The professor builds his premise for the program on a guess, by writing "what boys *seem* to need is the very thing they fear" (emphasis added). He indicates a desperate state of affairs, aspiring to save boys and men, and society in general, from the damaging ethos of masculinity as it has been known throughout human history. So teaching a young boy to control his emotions, finding his equilibrium between the extremes, is interpreted as "the earliest stirrings of a male identity at war with itself," with "devastating consequences" for "thin-skinned males," such that "young men suffer beneath the gravity of conventional masculinity."

Contrasting girls' increasing college enrollment during an 18-year stretch with boys' unchanging levels and underperformance in the classroom, the author lays blame on a deteriorating pathology of traditional masculinity. Too bad there was no investigation of a *real* pathology, manifested by family breakdown, male unemployment and incarceration, all of which result in absentee fathers, or the pedagogy used throughout primary and secondary schools. Neither could one witness a discussion about how absent male role models deny boys the opportunity to learn virtuous masculinity, or about the potential benefit from single-sex classrooms. Fundamentally, we must challenge the classification of "poor behavior," knowing the modern rejection of traditional values of "virtue" and "masculinity" has reinterpreted their associated behaviors as "poor."

How wonderful to imagine a return of the "Academy" and its scholarship, to once again learn about virtuous manhood as exemplified by the selfless heroism of Quasimodo, the perseverance of Augustine, and the moral excellence of Aristotle, along with the STEM courses. But that dream has been replaced by the reality of degrees in "Victim" Studies of gender, race and politics…or Golf Management.

Conclusion

Over the past few decades, the academic performance and moral strength of many American students have significantly declined, with the greatest change occurring in boys. This decline is evident when compared with American students of prior generations and with their international peers. Turning this trend around will be difficult at best because the primary causes—family breakdown, educational sloth, moral decay and relativism—show no sign of improving. Additionally, an infrastructure of many "experts" has been built by the public school system in order to help the "victims"—at the expense of boys. But neither those experts nor the billions of tax dollars supporting their efforts have helped—and the decline continues. With so much money at stake there would seem to be little incentive to correct the problem. But certain changes would help:

- Lesson plans should be based upon new data about boys' brains.
- Lesson plans could incorporate computer gaming teams, including regular associated outdoor activities with these teams.
- Political correctness in any manifestation should be banished, and constitutionally protected speech and action should be restored.
- Incentivize males to the teaching profession, helping to pay for it by reducing administrative bloat, union stranglehold and shared municipal services.
- Employ aspects of the Academy and its Classical Tradition, including holistic, physical culture programs, single-sex programs and moral excellence.

But the most critical change to be made is for parents—especially fathers—to choose their children's well-being over their own by doing the following:

- Remain married, except for extreme circumstances.
- Confirm the dignity and self-worth of their children, and shape it with discipline and moral virtue.
- Assert their role as the primary teacher of their children.

By following these guidelines, our children can learn to use more of their brain and have a greater chance of success—in every aspect of their lives.

According to Joseph Campbell, to be successful in one's journey, each must "confront and be initiated by whatever holds the ultimate power in his life." For most boys, that force should be his father. The success during each step of the journey leads one to the next, until the fullness of the journey is attained at the end. But today, the poor behavior of too many fathers makes me believe that, instead, we should atone for our sins toward our sons. So the most important change needed applies to every aspect of this book: we men need to use our will to make a simple choice, resolving to become the responsible and virtuous mentors all boys need. This mentoring should be a combination of formal structure, often with the random fun of a game.

CHAPTER 11

The Hard Knocks of Becoming Number One

My father used to play with my brother and me in the yard. Mother would come out and say, "You're tearing up the grass"; "We're not raising grass," Dad would reply. "We're raising boys."

—Harmon Killebrew

THE VALUE IN ANY TRIUMPH is commensurate with the importance of the challenge and the truthfulness of the competition. The hero's journey spurns mediocrity but welcomes and rewards extraordinary effort and service given to others. Absent a struggle for a noble purpose, living and dying offer neither the opportunity for glory nor chance for real freedom to discover truth. What remains is an involuntary, passive, and passionless existence. Today's awards for the commonplace are false honors. A slight loss from slight commitment is less honorable than a profound loss after the hero has given everything from the deepest recesses of his being. His reward, even in defeat, is that he lived fully—and truthfully—in every aspect.

Too many of our boys are not suffering even slight losses, because either they do not enter the contest or aren't allowed to suffer. Supervising their artificial contests, adults keep the specter of defeat—and all its lessons—at bay, attempting to boost self-esteem by making sure every contestant "wins." Boys therefore never breach the limits of comfort—and don't think they need to. But the reckoning will come.

But how can boys ever earn true victory, a knighthood duly earned, if they have never been provoked into doing so or have received no preparation for the competition? Their unwillingness or, more likely, inability to rise up and meet the great challenges diminishes themselves to themselves, reinforcing the limits on them they already presumed. And their loss is also our loss, because any potential benefit to mankind from their journey is never realized, since no journey was completed. Fortunate is the boy who understands the fraud of these vain "contests," is sufficiently disturbed by the emptiness of his "wins" and is therefore impelled to look for the truth in the results of competition—and in himself.

This false existence is what often passes for the competitive life of American boys. Too much of it is superficial, lacks commitment, and shackles boys in compromise and comfort. They have no heroes, because none are needed in a life without challenge. When they see evidence of heroic behavior, they feel an aching emptiness, and long for the day they might, just might, demonstrate heroism. But how will they accomplish this if their role models are missing? How can a boy learn this if he has no men of virtue to teach him? Having been abandoned, either willfully or in ignorance, they grow up without maturing and are woefully incomplete. How sad. One aspect of the current opioid abuse crisis rarely explored is arguably the most important: the spiritual void within many men from a lack of purpose and meaning—and perhaps a loving dad. They somehow need to know that the world needs them, and their virtue.

Father & Son Playtime is Vital

The ideal introduction for this valuable education typically begins with the loving roughhousing that dads are best equipped to do. This is a preparatory phase, something I regularly did with Kevin not very long after his birth. This phase is, of course, important, since much of who we become is due to seeds planted at a very early age, in the form of varied behaviors and interactions. So, heroes and superheroes were welcomed in our home, and Kevin couldn't wait to become one.

My son and I played countless games as Batman, Spiderman, and the like, creating endless schemes in each one. I was always on the side of evil, a role I played with such relish and grandeur that it invariably drove him to attack me at the conclusion, the two of us wrestling in the climactic battle. When father and son share this active play toys may be scattered, but the formation that occurs makes it less likely a boy's identity will be similarly strewn.

Authorities on this subject, such as Steve Biddulph and James Dobson, support activity such as this. Biddulph, author of *Raising Boys*, relates part of this to the increased levels of boys' testosterone, which is when they become most interested in "action, heroics, adventures and vigorous play." And whether the son succeeds or fails, the father often sees the outcome as an indicator of *his* level of effectiveness. This is true with most aspects of life.

Dobson has written much on the subject, one being his best-selling book, *Bringing Up Boys*. This work parallels some of Biddulph's, and it speaks bluntly about the competitive physicality of boys and why it is normal. "Why are they like this?" Dobson asks, and then answers, "Some would say their mischievous nature has been learned from the culture. Really? Then why are boys more aggressive in every society around the globe?"

More than a Game

It's normal for a son to want to emulate his father, then achieve from what he has learned in order to become his own man. This is nature's progression, and should be encouraged and brought forth. Accomplishing this involves a variety of skills typically learned during a boy's ongoing experiences under his father's careful tutelage.

Thus, a boy is shaped into a man partly by identifying with his father and his father's mannerisms. He'll learn his father's voice, postures, and bearing, and how they change according to experiences he has with men, women, and children; and he'll learn kindness when he sees that in his father. Men who did not have these experiences can certainly make great achievements in spite of an absent, uninvolved, or mean father, but that journey will be more difficult to successfully complete. And whatever their successes, they will still have the incompleteness from the deficient father.

Early on, Kevin was frequently engaged in a variety of challenges, particularly those related to school and athletics. He was always competitive and very much wanted to win. These games were always enjoyable and done in a spirit of good will. However, when it was time to engage *me* in a contest, especially one of a physical nature, my son brought his intensity to a noticeably high level. That came as no surprise because he had, after all, the biology of a boy. If the contest ended because of time, he would always have difficulty acknowledging the clock. He, of course, wanted to beat me. I was glad for that, and welcomed that eventuality—all in good time, of course!

Toward the end of summer going into sixth grade, Kevin had to undergo hernia surgery. This greatly reduced his activity for many weeks, and perhaps the biggest limitation was his inability to wrestle with me. This activity started when he was very young, and we called it "sumo." I cannot describe exactly the form we used over the subsequent years because it was a fusion of many techniques, but I'm confident that every once in a while a move would have been recognizable to the American Wrestling Association. The rest was "come as what may." His injury was the first time we were so restricted and limited and we didn't like it.

Most of our activities were great fun, but still my thoughts were of the hopes of pushing Kevin toward independence. One contest that particularly stands out occurred during the summer after his high school freshman year.

Our family was enjoying, once again, a vacation in Vermont, where the temperate weather always enabled us to explore that beautiful state and engage in many outdoor activities. On this trip we rented a quaint farmhouse, and from there traveled around to enjoy events and sceneries so easy to find in that state. But one day, my wife and daughter convinced me we needed a vacation from the vacation, and we decided to enjoy a leisurely day on our rented farm. The farmer's wife recommended a game of croquet, and so we followed her advice as well as her explanation of the rules. Their lush lawn was the court and the stunning Green Mountains the backdrop.

Croquet began as a sport for the refined set, the upper crust of society, and was at first a game for royalty. But had they witnessed the "match within a match" that eventually unfolded between Kevin and me, they would know we had more in common with the great unwashed of our land than with the courtly gentlemen who invented the game.

The match progressed with knocks and scores and all were having fun, including the farmer's wife, who acted as the rules advisor. Although I saw Kevin sharing the laughs, I noticed changes in my son's demeanor, changes not evident in either my wife or my daughter. For example, he took more time to line up his shots, reacted more vigorously to those shots and to mine, and would stare at me with an intensity that suggested victory was at least as important as good humor. But heaven forbid any of the rest of us took too long (in Kevin's mind) to take our shots, or we'd hear about it.

While the gentler sex gave their best effort, they were, sadly, eliminated. My wife was first to go, and uttered "Darn!" before laughing and walking to the sideline. But my daughter took it a little harder. She dropped her little blond head at the same time she dropped her mallet, and silently walked away, sad that her involvement in the croquet "party" was finished. Thankfully this devastation was short lived because her attention was quickly drawn to the farm kitten's futile, but never-ending, chase after a fluttering moth. Off she bounded with shrieks of joy in an effort to aid the kitty, innocent of the fact she was terrifying both it and the moth. Her devastation of a moment ago disappeared.

Their departure left to my son and me the honor and burden of finishing this game, and of doing so in a manner respectful of the royalty that invented it. For the next half hour, we seemed to be doing just that. Our contest appeared to be a friendly and gentlemanly rivalry, with each of us complimenting the other. Eventually, I noticed that only my compliments were clearly audible while Kevin's became more subdued. As much as I knew I was his mentor, I should have realized my son saw me as his competitor, an opponent trying to keep him from victory. As the game developed, it became apparent this would become a mano-a-mano struggle for supremacy. Kevin's stern countenance reflected his determination. He had to win, and he had to best his father.

As the contest progressed toward the inevitable finish there was an occasional smile, but the intensity increased as we wondered which ball would arrive first at the ultimate destination. So, we spent more time lining up our shots and then groan whenever the wicket was missed; but his were louder than mine. The muscle activity of his hands and forearms seemed to intensify his grip on the mallet, making me think this match may not end in the aforementioned refined and dignified manner. Periodically I would have him in a vulnerable position, but his clutch shots prevented my victory. His fist pumps were accompanied by a "Yes!" suggesting the importance of this match. Once I pondered, "Should I let him win so he can feel good about himself?" "No way" was my immediate reply.

I rightly sensed this game was about much more than croquet. It was about my son reaching and stretching for his independence, and then shedding more of his father's restraints while dropping the "daddy" in favor of the more mature "dad."

The match was a step on his journey from boyhood in a raw quest to become a man. This progression is completely normal and should be celebrated and encouraged. Manhood is not built on falsehood. Only a true victory would be good for Kevin, so I could not hand it to him. He would know it, and would not be able to grow himself upon a false triumph. The Masai teenager would not have his victory over the antelope, lion, or himself if the elders eased the requirements by, say, entrapping or drugging the animal he was to kill. A man produced by such a watered-down ritual would be of little use to the village and unable to teach others. If he loses, but did so valiantly, he would have the moral victory that many dismiss. A boy's peers won't let him win, so I let the battle unfold…

As play continued upon the farm's rich turf and we neared the end, Kevin inadvertently struck the ball so that it ended up in front of an open wicket, and suddenly I was on the threshold of certain triumph. The pained look on his face reflected great dismay.

During my pause we lifted our heads and met each other's gaze, and then with an air of bravado and nonchalance, I tapped mallet to ball in the final, victorious shot.

As the ball passed through the final arch and slowed to a stop, the grass resumed its upright position—as did I. Time seemed suspended as if in respectful acknowledgment of my victory. I then turned and looked at Kevin. The pained smile on his face reflected resigned acceptance of my victory, and I humorously basked in my conquest. Future historians will surely note that my next move was the spark that ignited Kevin's combative flame and caused what turned out to be the *actual* conclusion of our "match."

After several seconds of glowing, and continuing to look at my vanquished son, I cavalierly opened my hand to drop the mallet, not caring where it would land. And why would I? The contest was over and I no longer needed my weapon. I had won and he hadn't. I was still on top, and my posture indicated this. Inside I was enjoying the humor, but only briefly. Kevin knew my sense of humor, and our many sporting "battles" this humor encouraged. Anger never played a part. So it was on this day. Nevertheless, the intensity level remained high. The arc of the mallet's fall was gradual, but gravity had its way.

A second after the mallet landed my son bolted from his stance twenty feet away, hurtling 145 pounds of testosterone-charged determination my way. It was as if my dropping of the mallet was a red cape to a young bull, or an insult that called for a duel. It wasn't pistols at forty paces but a collision from twenty. My eyes widened in anticipation, and I had only enough time for a brief laugh before closing my eyes and to brace for contact.

The manner of the clash and the loud grunts it brought forth recalled our sumo days, but both the lack of sofa cushions and the size and strength of my son promptly ended that reminiscence. By this time Kevin had a year of football, wrestling and powerlifting under his belt, and he began working me with arms and legs in a manner suggesting he had more than two of each. During the early part of this contest I enjoyed some laughs, but eventually all that could be heard were grunts, growls, and the sounds of bodies grappling and feet jostling.

A Boy for All Seasons, but a Man...?

Although I was athletic and fit, Kevin had me at a disadvantage because, unlike me, he wasn't thinking of any consequences and went full bore. The battle was on, and that was all that mattered to him. He was like an animal, existing in an intense presence. We strained and struggled with flexed muscles and taut tendons, letting out bursts of breath and snorts. On one or two occasions I tried to make him laugh in an effort to throw off his game; but the best I could get was a hint of a smile. All this time I could faintly hear my wife yelling for us to stop, but this contest needed to be concluded.

Unbeknown to my son and me, one side of the playing field was on the edge of a steep hill, and those watching saw we were veering precariously toward it, unaware. I lunged, trying for his leg and a takedown, and seemed to be on the verge of a second victory that day. But before I could stand he countered from on top by looping his right arm around my head and neck, and then from that headlock grabbed my wrist with his right hand. I didn't know it at the time, but he was preparing me for the notorious "cement mixer," an appropriately titled move because of how one is twisted to one's back in a helpless position. Since he had my neck in his unthinking hands, I would, in all likelihood, have to go wherever his arms decided. But he couldn't pull it off because of my greater size and strength, and I broke free.

We resumed the contest and maneuvered our bodies to end this epic battle. Kevin kept trying to outfox me, but I continued to parry his efforts. Suddenly, my neck and head were grabbed in a move so unorthodox that I am sure the Vermont State Legislature has since outlawed it. As Kevin's grip tightened and I was fighting him off, we lost our balance as the ground fell out from underneath—into nothing. We had unknowingly maneuvered ourselves to that sharp slope of the farmer's property. For a second there was only air.

Upon our jarring landing, everyone heard the three popping sounds emanating from my neck—a kind that would have crowned a chiropractic career. We both released our respective grips, Kevin out of concern for me and I from self-preservation. At that point we ended the match with our clothes grass-stained, egos maintained, and, number-one status still held by Dad, albeit a bit bruised in the process. It was with great relief I realized I could feel all my limbs. The match within a match was one for the ages.

The Mentor Model

I realized Kevin's growth, coupled with his improving strength and skills, made it increasingly likely that the only way I could beat him in the future was if I were prepared to go all out—which of course I would never do.

Since that day I've often thought of that match, in part because of the hearty laughs that resulted, but also because it was such a telling day for me about my son. I was the standard against which he was measuring himself. He was like the young male dog determined to test me for alpha status, which is good and completely normal as long as it is done with respect for the old dog. On that day he gave me, as he has ever since, a run for my money. So I knew he was following the natural law, moving forward in his efforts to be better—than me, his peers, and, most importantly, himself at each step.

Kevin was moving through his initiation phase of the hero's journey; at the step Campbell calls "atonement (at-one-ment) with the father." As the journey of manhood progresses, the boy will see his father from a different perspective and understand him better, because he has a better understanding of himself. At that point the two have become one with each other. That is how it is supposed to be but sadly often isn't, mainly due to the mistakes of the father. But if a mentor steps in to fill that void, then the boy has a better chance to successfully complete his journey. I gave thanks for that, also for the fact we were able to have these "training" experiences, because they helped him mature.

So that croquet/wrestling match was both fun and serious. It affirmed for Kevin that he was sufficiently important to me because I wanted to have this experience with him, and that I had confidence in his ability to handle himself without my direction. More importantly, events like the post-game contest made Kevin increasingly confident to reach further in his exploration beyond his assumed boundaries—and then help others do the same for themselves.

It is crucial to a boy's normal development that he and his dad—or another caring mentor—also share a variety of challenging as well as enjoyable experiences, even though these activities sometimes involve an element of danger. For example, when swimming in the ocean, the son may be a bit anxious or fearful in the beginning; but when the boy sees the father is having fun, he gains confidence and begins to have fun himself. The joy felt from these experiences is increased by the regular encouragement the son receives from his father, such that it personifies that relationship and becomes important to the natural formation of a boy's masculine identity.

Ross Parke, psychologist from University of California at Riverside, wrote, "Attempts to understand the 'active ingredient' in fathers' play, revealed that children learn critical lessons about how to recognize and deal with highly charged emotions in the context of playing with their fathers…Fathers, in effect, give children practice in regulating their own emotions and recognizing others' emotional cues." This, and similar findings in other research, would make it logical to conclude that the presence of good fathers and mentors in boys' lives help those boys have fewer psychological problems. And their presence in family life also has a similar effect on their daughters.

Several years later while Kevin was in college, he came to me and said he wanted to buy a motorcycle with money he had earned. I raised the usual objections for all the right reasons, but didn't say no. Unbeknown to me, he subsequently bought it. I knew he had earned the money and an implicit consent from me that would stretch and grow both of us. Kevin had the confidence to make this decision, and would be responsible for everything about the bike—including the insurance to pay for college if interrupted by injury or death. My responsibility was to let go of my son.

A boy needs to hear a good man talk, and to learn the measure of those words and the timbre of the voice behind them. He needs to see a good man carry himself, and to understand the posture, gestures, and movements required of a man. A boy needs to have a good man patiently listen to him express important things about himself and his life, and know he has been understood and valued. A boy also needs to see humility in a good man who has fallen along the way from poor judgment, but who then arises to recover his virtue in his service to others. That virtue is the source of true joy.

Being a "good man" is the father's challenge because he wants to teach the boy how to navigate the roads ahead in order to maximize the successes and minimize the failures. He should know his own experiences, and the good and bad judgments he used throughout his life. The boy eventually has to take the wheel—or handlebars—and drive by himself. A good mentor reduces the chances for devastating crashes along the way, and increases the likelihood the boy will reach his destination and fulfill his purpose: that of a life well lived for himself and for others. Today, far too many of our boys are behind the wheel, with no idea how to drive let alone avoid opposing traffic—especially involving relationships.

CHAPTER 12

The Birds and the Bees and the Boys

O Lord, grant me chastity, but not yet.

—SAINT AUGUSTINE

"GUYS! LISTEN UP!" BOOMED MR. Disanza. The stocky ninth-grade physical education teacher barked his instructions like the Marine tank commander he used to be. We listened, not wanting to experience any more of the raw power he exuded. Although not tall, he was broad of chest and shoulders, and had thickly muscled extremities. His big neck must have made buying shirts a terrific challenge, perhaps giving him another good reason to teach Health & Physical Education since ties were never needed. His military rank made sense because he looked like a tank and was in full command of both his body and his classes.

This was 1970, and we were in the waning stage of the hippie culture, so boys' hair was still long and pocket combs a necessity—but not for this teacher, since he wore his high and tight. This would be the class of '74's first sex education class, and he wanted to restore some order out of the chaos in the minds and bodies of the adolescent males in front of him.

Prior to arriving in the classroom, most of the boys were in an enthused state, something that increased the closer each of them got to the room. The bumping, shoving, and innocent casualties seemed to scatter bodies on the mad dash to most boys' favorite class. They ignored the calls by the hall monitor to "walk, don't run!", each having had the great expectation that by passing through the classroom door he was entering a school-sanctioned Shangri-La, one that would bring him closer to understanding the great mystery: sex! This would be the only class whose textbook boys would be happy to read, with some whipping through the pages in search of "educational" pictures.

Once we dropped into our seats, the teacher barked his orders and the buzzing conversation ceased. Chalk in hand, he turned and began his blackboard art, drawings meant to be serious representations of the procreative organs of the two sexes. Serious attempts perhaps, but the snickering response they elicited suggested an unsophisticated audience, which is, by definition, a group of teenaged boys.

"Hey, Mr. D!" one boy called out, using the name by which our teacher was affectionately known. "I never saw an elephant with a trunk that small!" Amid the laughter, another responded with the follow-up dig no boy wants to receive: "Nah, he must have seen Billy coming out of the locker room shower." As the giggling and embarrassment faded, Mr. D smiled, maybe thinking that boys' interest in this subject must go way back, perhaps to humanity's beginning.

Upon reaching puberty, boys are notorious for having a fascination about sex and a tendency to joke about it. Perhaps during their early years, some of the men reading this book received a subscription to *National Geographic Kids*, as I had from my aunt and uncle when I was twelve years old. I recall opening the first issue, and my startled reaction at seeing photographs of partially naked tribal African women. Whichever chemicals were firing inside my male brain upon seeing these images, were certainly unknown to me. And I do not recall if my obligatory thank you note to my relatives was unusually enthusiastic. This teenage interest can focus on sexuality, anatomy, or sexual activity. The fascination probably arises because the subject is intensely private, personal and restricted, and makes teenagers (and all of us, really) so utterly vulnerable.

That vulnerability is one big reason why romance should never be liberated from virtue, but manifestly has been since the sexual revolution of the 1960s. As this pseudo-liberation widened during my teenage years, due largely to increasing contraception and decreasing morality, we increasingly detached our genitalia from their purpose as well as the good and noble harmony with the rest of our bodies. These changes occurred simultaneously with the rise of the divorce culture, and with the absence of any ritual to formally usher boys into manhood.

As their sexuality comes of age, boys need the most guidance in developing the virtuous perspective about both the mechanics and its purpose; but all too often they do not get any, and are left susceptible to questionable substitutes such as ignorant peers and schools. The results are often disastrous.

I am Roman Catholic from birth, and my first experience of the barest hint of romance occurred in fourth grade, and with it my first moral dilemma. I found myself attracted to…a nun! Considering my early age, the attraction reached only to the most superficial parts of my brain. Still, Sister John Maura (it was common practice for religious sisters, and nuns, to take the name of a male saint) had a face of raw beauty and cheery disposition, features that contrasted sharply with the severe demeanor and behavior of my third-grade teacher. The previous year's experience had been difficult, largely due to the clash of personalities with my teacher, so trouble was no stranger to me.

Just prior to the start of fourth grade, I learned that my new teacher had specifically arranged for me to be in her class, determined, was she, to help me flourish. She was to be my "Sister Benedict," like the disciplined, caring and beautiful nun played by Ingrid Bergman in *The Bells of Saint Mary's*, and she would go on to give me both the encouragement and guidance I needed. I'm sure that was a big reason for my good feelings toward her. Despite the passage of decades, those good feelings remain because her noble efforts had the intended salutary effects on me. I eventually learned she did not remain a bride of Christ, and thought perhaps she had become a bride of some blessed man.

Elvira

During those eight years of elementary school, my brief experiences with sex "education" involved experts such as Brian, a neighbor who shocked me one day in the back room of our family's old barn with a few "dirty pictures," making me, indeed, feel dirty; and by Elvira (yes, that was her real name, by way of Tuscany rather than Tennessee), a resident of Saint Mary's Orphanage in nearby Newark, New Jersey, and the first girl to kiss me on the lips. This event occurred underneath an old gas lamppost along a street not far from my home, and ushered in the official start of romance manifesting itself in my life.

Leading up to the kiss, I had become aware she was paying more attention to me in school, as she would occasionally touch my arm or hand while making a point and sometimes let that touch linger. The first time this happened, I became aware of a very strange feeling coursing through me, one that was simultaneously pleasant and disorienting—considering I was all of twelve years old. Although she was in the same grade as I, Elvira was three years older (no doubt held back by obvious turmoil in her life). So considering how females mature earlier, I was a mere babe in the woods to her wily romantic ways.

On this eventful day, I walked the mile or so from my house to the orphanage to meet Elvira and go for a walk. I recall being more than a bit nervous, largely because this was the first time I was walking to meet a girl. *"What do I say?"* I thought. *"What am I supposed to do?"* These thoughts repeated themselves along with my increasing anxiety. By that age, I had received plenty of instructions on how to hit a baseball and shoot a basketball, and I was well versed in Catholic prayers, including the Act of Contrition, one that expresses sorrow for sins and a commitment to be better—which I thought I might especially need after this meeting with Elvira. But conversation with a girl—about romance—might as well have been a foreign language to me.

My experience with girls up to that point had come mostly from living with my four sisters, an arrangement that was intermittently harmonious because of the varying levels of maturity. Walking to the homes of my friends was the norm, requiring no anxiety or contemplation of what we would say or do because a ball game was always in the making. After the games, we would periodically talk about the girls in our classes, but to paraphrase the great wisdom of Father Bobby Lennon, the uncle of my friend Chris Tivenan, we were "just exchanging ignorances." But Elvira and I were not going to play basketball.

Upon arriving at my destination, I saw Elvira waiting on the front porch of the red brick building. She was wearing a floral dress with lots of light blue in it, as well as a wide grin, partly at seeing me and partly from enjoying the surprised stares of the other orphan girls—of which there were many. I could see them through the iron bars bordering the large property, others looking out the many windows of the large building. It was strange to me, coming from a normal home. I felt sympathy for them, knowing they were not part of the family of their birth and wondering what each could have been thinking about that. These thoughts made me glad to know that I lived on the other side of those bars, and that I had a family to which I would soon return—no matter how annoying each of us could be to the others!

We started walking along the busy South Orange Avenue, and when she grabbed my hand to hold during that walk, I again had that feeling of pleasant confusion moving through me, along with a pounding heart and a very dry mouth. It was unnerving because it was mysterious to me. I was feeling, but not comprehending, the barest beginning of romantic love, or eros. And it wouldn't be until many years later that I would only begin to unravel part of that mystery. Hesiod, one of the earliest Greek poets, described Eros as being "fairest among the gods, who unnerves the limbs and overcomes the mind."

Along the way, Elvira would hold my hand, and then my arm, contrasting for me the warmth of her hands with the ice of mine. She seemed relaxed in her gait and comfortable with her talk. I recall none of the actual conversation but do remember I initially had great difficulty forming words. In all likelihood I had, just prior to this meeting, been confidently rattling off to my friends some statistics about the Green Bay Packers or New York Yankees—but this was different. Lacking any experience, I could therefore draw on neither memories nor instructions for guidance. This dearth of information, coupled with a parched mouth, made conversation a challenge.

We turned off the noisy avenue to take a shortcut through quiet neighborhoods, those with old Victorian houses, large oak and beech trees, and high hedgerows. I wondered if she imagined what it was like to live in one of those houses, with a mother, father and siblings, rather than in her "home." I never learned why she was an orphan, probably because I hadn't the maturity to ask. Eventually we ended up at the lamppost on Center Street, where the talking ceased.

Up until that time, I had never felt awkward at the end of a conversation because every one of them concluded with a mutual good-bye. But when we turned toward each other she didn't say good-bye. And the abrupt silence from one who'd been so chatty throughout our meandering walk was unsettling. I saw that her brown eyes were moving side to side, intently focusing upon each of my eyes in a manner that immobilized me. Then I realized her face was, ever so slowly, moving toward mine, while at the same time her eyelids were gently lowering. I realized I, too, was being drawn toward her, compelled by a force over which I seemed to have no control. And it was the first time I did not want to turn my head in either direction. It felt as I might imagine feeling after having fallen off a steep cliff, but with the security of an embrace by one who's done it before—and who enjoyed it. The touch of our lips was like nothing I could have imagined. I felt as though I was continuously descending into layers of a softness that seemed to have no end.

Thinking back, I'm sure I was echoing a reaction to history's first kiss, an event whose origin we of course don't know, but historical records shed light on the special meaning of the kiss. The ancient Hindu Vedas provide what is perhaps the earliest record of kissing, dating back to approximately 1500 BC. In these texts, kissing is inferred by references to "drinking moisture of the lips." Early Christians were known to exchange an *osculum pacis* (holy kiss of peace), an indication of spirit transmission from one to the other.

Since Elvira was of Italian ancestry and female, the kiss was immediately followed by an affectionate, tender hug. It was pure emotion. Being of Irish lineage, a boy, and only twelve, my eyes were as open as hers were closed during that hug, and I wondered what all this meant. My stomach was behaving in a way previously unknown to me. In an instant I knew at least one meaning it would have, because in the middle of that hug I saw my family's car go by, driven by my mother with one of my older brothers as her passenger. They both smiled, but only one of those smiles was kind and had good intent. I knew perfectly well that the motivation behind Marty's smile was completely different from the innocent, loving, and, yes, surprised one from my mother. My brother was no doubt enjoying my embarrassment and this new source of leverage he now had on me. He has been quite successful in his career of high finance, leveraging one thing against another, and I've no doubt that the seeds of those skills were planted at a young age, often at the expense of his younger brother.

When the hug with Elvira finally ended, she grabbed my hand and expressed her desire to remain with me rather than go back to the orphanage. Having been baptized and confirmed by the Holy Spirit, I was filled with the associated Sacramental graces, but my relative youth made me ignorant about the social graces needed to converse with a girl, generally, and especially one I had just kissed.

She smiled at my incoherent expressions, misinterpreting them as evidence of my having been love-struck, when in fact I had actually been struck dumb by the experience—and had no desire to remain with her. But I did say I did not wish to go home, leaving her to imagine that my reasoning was the same as hers. What I left unspoken was the simple fact that I knew Marty would make sure the news of my embrace would be all over the house, and therefore didn't want to endure interview requests from any of my seven siblings. Ultimately I said I had to go home, no doubt in a clumsy manner.

Although Elvira and I lived not far from each other, I altered my route home so this "relationship" would have no chance of developing. Fortunately for me, the school year would soon be ending, as would my time in Our Lady of Sorrows, and Elvira and I were never to meet again. It's funny now to recall the day during fifth grade when my father, fresh from seeing a poor report card of mine, threatened to send me to that very same orphanage if I didn't straighten out. Little did either of us know that in a few years I probably would have welcomed the exile—at least for a while.

So the aforementioned experiences were my early education about sex and romance as an activity, and it was paltry compared to what I learned about history or math. I heard more about "masculine" and "feminine" during grammar lessons in both English and Spanish than at any other time throughout high school. I wish I had learned more, because that may have prevented some of my later troubles. But I take some solace knowing many before me went through the same difficulties.

THE TIMELESS CHALLENGE

The epigraph to this chapter suggests that Saint Augustine could rightly be called the patron saint of teenage boys and young men. In *Confessions*, his semi-autobiographical magnum opus to God of confession, prayer and praise, he reminisces—often in obvious pain—about his progression into a period of lust-filled adolescence and early adulthood, and the shame that behavior brought to him and his family. As Book II unfolds he writes, "I will try now to give a coherent account of my *disintegrated* [emphasis added] self, for when I turned away from you…God…I went to pieces." (We'll revisit *disintegration* later in this chapter.) Augustine clearly and courageously expresses his shame, grief and regret at the results of his inability and, worse, unwillingness, to control his sexuality. These are feelings many of us can share. And it seems easy to sympathize with his delight in the beauty of this world, "For there is an attractiveness in beautiful bodies, in gold and silver, and all things; and in bodily touch, sympathy has much influence."

He admits the unfortunate influence of some friends and succumbing to peer pressure in a way that anybody today could understand—whether or not he committed the sin—because he wanted to fit in; "I would say that I had done what I had not done, that I might not seem contemptible [to his friends]." But during his flagrant periods when he committed the offending deed, there was no guilt, saying, "It was foul, and I loved it." Guilt would come later.

As he grew into adulthood and progressed toward the religious life, Augustine still struggled, pouring those difficulties into his writings when describing, say, the chaste life of his mentor, Bishop Ambrose. He refers to Ambrose's choice of celibacy as a "painful burden." Further on he describes his own pain at the idea of a life without romance, whether or not that included a covenantal marriage, "I sought not being so much a lover of marriage as a slave to lust." He fretted with great misery at the prospect of never again experiencing the feminine touch, saying, "I thought I should be too miserable, unless folded in female arms." Made weak from his struggles with romance, he referred to his desires as "an infirmity." Augustine's struggle was, in part, related to the commitment to celibacy that his ordination—which he resisted—foreshadowed.

Lest any young men reading this dare conclude that sexual adventurism is the first step toward sainthood, Augustine describes the strong grip his "reckless desire" had on him, one he would eventually overcome through what proved to be his greatest relationship—with God. His conversion, however, was a process years in the making.

Having lived sixteen centuries ago, his writings suggest the timeless challenge sex, romance, and love have been to adolescent boys and young men, each group having the initial challenge of understanding the manifestations of their biology and the associated masculine gender. Virtually every fetus will be born male or female and will express this in the behavior (inborn and learned) for which they are designed. And this helps form our identity. But unlike animals, we are thinking, self-aware beings who are not compelled to act upon instinct. So we should learn about our nature and how best to fulfill it—with judicious control.

Yet, this presents a problem. It is difficult to imagine how we can learn this responsibility about sexuality when most of us get little or no training in such a fundamental part of life. Augustine's writings could make one think that he, too, had little parental involvement in this matter, particularly from his father, as indicated by his description of an event in his sixteenth year in his ongoing conversation with God: "When my father saw me at the (public) baths, now growing towards manhood he…already anticipating his descendants, gladly told it to my mother; rejoicing in that tumult of the senses wherein the world forgot its Creator. But yet this same father had no concern how I grew towards Thee (God), or how chaste I were."

Romantic love, known in antiquity as Eros, the god of procreation, is the chemistry that drives us toward each other. In that literature, a youthful Eros is described as the mischievous and disobedient god of sensual love, whose purpose is to spur creation by lighting the flame of love in the hearts of men and women. Joseph Campbell describes this as an impersonal love, which makes sense since Eros is, at times, depicted as having his eyes covered as he acts blindly. That would be bad enough for the modern boy, but today it is much worse because of what he would see if the blindfold were to be removed. And the ramifications are ominous.

Since Augustine's time, there have been countless boys who have shared experiences similar to those about which he wrote. The greater challenge for us today comes from living in a culture that celebrates near-complete sexual freedom, but does so in a misunderstanding of "love" from having neither the guidance of an intact family nor the wisdom from a religious faith. In fact, it is the absence of those two factors that has loosened the bridles traditionally used to help one attempt to control one's sexual life. And the enticements aren't over.

The Eyes Have It

During my weekly business trips to Manhattan, I must frequently avert my eyes from the pull of eros—that is, from the advertisers' images of women (and, sadly, girls). They are meant to evoke the aforementioned "uncontrollable desire" for that product and perhaps the associated erotica. The provocative postures, facial expressions, and makeup are the ancient tools of temptation and seduction, and make these women seem the temptresses of which Campbell described.

But how could advertisers and other purveyors of sexual stimuli throughout time have known how effective this carnal imagery would be? After all, it is only recently that brain scans and chemical analyses have provided evidence that the male brain responds much differently to visual sexual stimuli than the female brain, and does so in a way similar to that of the animal brain. It must have been the result of eons of observation of human behavior. So in all likelihood "advertisers," from Antiquity, must have always known the effectiveness of sexual imagery upon males. However, advertisers, too, have been liberated, and today's culture not only permits greater license, but also demands it.

Acting like a reflex, this apparent arousal response is evoked from the brain circuitry, flaming the pilot light of eros that burns in the background of men. When not restrained, this flicker can become an uncontrollable blaze. During the last half century, how many women involved in advertising considered this objectification of their sex, but then protested when their work proved to stimulate in men more than just the desire for the advertised item? While objecting to the inappropriate *actions* of men who acted on those desires would be justifiable, any offense at the *desire* would be both unreasonable and hypocritical.

But this hypocrisy is just another area in which adults play the youthful game of "Pretend", trying to convince each other that an obvious reality and the truth behind it is actually something else. We pretend males shouldn't have these initial reactions to the female body, reactions that are hardwired in biology for procreation, and which must be managed through self-control. Why do we expect this change when it has never occurred in human history?

Many women, including evangelical Christians, object to the "modesty equals dignity" argument, asserting that it is up to men to not objectify women however they are dressed. Our cultural changes make this reaction unsurprising, even with those of a professed traditional religious affiliation. But considering the point made in the previous paragraphs about brain chemistry and the eons of human behavior, it is hard to imagine a reality upon which these opinions could be based. While a mature response from a man's rational brain is the correct one, it only comes *after* the immediate physiologic reaction from the more primitive brain. Any time I see those sirens during my midtown walks, I have no idea what is lighting up in my brain. And I sometimes wonder about the thoughts those women had during the time surrounding the photo shoot.

Considering the potential harm from uninhibited sensuality, it should be self-evident that a boy's primary education about sex shouldn't be about gratuitous sexual stimulation. But that was exactly the purpose of those "dirty" photos I saw. For too many men and, increasingly, boys, this stimulation is the source of addictive behavior, releasing powerful neurotransmitters in our brains that result in a wonderful, narcotic-like effect—until our lives unravel as a terrible side effect.

The tragic irony is that, while pornography aims to stimulate us, it also desensitizes its victims to the mystery, romance, and love that should be a part of our mature sexuality. A big reason for that is the absence of any connection involving the physical, emotional and—especially—moral spirituality with the person being objectified, because it is a "virtual" experience. The viewer takes (in his mind) but can never give, as there is no "other" with whom he can complement in a relationship. Simply put, one cannot give anything—especially oneself—to a virtual "person." This is not the romantic and potentially honorable love of Eros, but the uncontrolled desire and unrequited love of Eros' troublemaking sibling, Himeros. Cultures preceding Christianity, including the Greeks, referred to this as a "divine madness," one that ultimately led to fertility cults where women who, having been drugged, were certainly not treated divinely—let alone humanely. These behaviors do not at all suggest prudence or justice, or any virtue for that matter, and portrays a way of life I could never imagine, most especially since the birth of Maureen.

The Father's Role with Daughters

With Kevin's birth I found a new kind of love, as I immediately realized how dependent he was upon me for protection, mentoring and modeling, and for the training that would enable him to secure his identity and seek his independence. We have shared so many wonderful experiences, and the blessings have been unending. I knew that while he would always have my love, devotion and blessing, he would eventually not need my protection. Maureen's arrival, on the other hand, brought forth a love of tenderness, endearment and protectiveness. Her dependence upon me to be *the* man in her life and to show her how other men should be toward her has been a great responsibility, but also an honor and blessing. The rewards have been unending, in part because she simply exudes for me her love and devotion. Ultimately, my love for both of them is unwavering, unending and accompanied by complete allegiance.

It has been twenty-three years since the joyous day of my daughter's birth, and my love for her has only grown. Maureen's profoundly loving nature has put me head over heels for her—forever. This love, combined with the shyness of her early years, helps to recall Wordsworth:

"The flower that smells the sweetest is shy and lowly."

While never lowly, Maureen was—and always will be—my sweetest flower. When she was much younger, she began writing notes to me that said, "I love you so much that I can't even say!" with the words surrounded by puffy drawings of many red and pink hearts. I absolutely love reading those messages, and have kept them. And I understood what she meant because I felt the same way. We still share that love, and always will. With that in mind, any mistreatment of her would make me want to mete out a severe penalty to that person. She has helped me be a better man in many ways, and I have learned from her to seek the dignity in every female.

In the situations described above, I have found Maureen to be a filter over my mind's eye. Ever since her birth I have seen women differently, often imagining them as having been their daddy's little girl and hoping those daddies loved them as much as I love Maureen. It is difficult for me to imagine otherwise, but easy to be sympathetic to daughters who did not have that love. Just as Maureen knows I wouldn't want anyone to disrespect her, I know she would expect me to be respectful with every female—because each is a child of God and therefore has intrinsic dignity. Having my daughter's respect is so very important, and I shudder to think of losing it. The thought of her looking away from me in shame or scorn rather than up to me with honor and pride has been an extremely powerful influence upon me.

Recently published research showed that quality fathering had a beneficial impact on the sexual behavior of daughters as compared to men who were detached and inattentive dads.[8] So, as imperfect as I am, I know that striving

---

8 DelPriore, Danielle J; Schlomer, Gabriel L; Ellis, Bruce J, "Impact of Fathers on Parental Monitoring of Daughters and Their Affiliation with Sexually Promiscuous Peers: A

to be a good man—remaining humble in my successes from the sting of past failures—will provide her with the best model of what to look for in a man who may one day be her husband. This pertains to her brother as well, leaving both Kevin and me with a big responsibility. It also leaves us with a big challenge, because cultural forces have left modesty in the dust.

The Modesty Virtue

Formally or not, a girl's presentation of herself for romantic relationships should be built upon maintaining her dignity and honor, as it should be with boys, and an early step in this process is the manner in which she dresses. But today's fashions have helped to devalue relationships. Rather than boys having hope for a romantic *relationship* from the peripheral hints of girls sensuality (via perfume, manner of speaking, or modestly revealing clothing), and then having to work as a moral craftsman or artist in order to bring that hope to reality in a committed (i.e., married) relationship, they now have the immediate expectation or demand for sex, based upon the strength of girls open display of their sexuality. And this is *before* the first drink. The nectar has been laid bare, drawing boys to the flower.

Today we meet much more easily and carelessly in a culture very different from the one that predominated only a few decades ago. But the culture consists of people and is what we make it, and we have made a mess. We have esteemed our children so much, and told them "yes" so often when the response should have been "no", that children feel they can have or do most anything they want—especially with sex, considering the desire for it.

The Christian tradition teaches the love of purity in all our relationships; prudence and common sense to guard it; and prayer and the grace to preserve it. Unfortunately, many of us want only our water to be pure. But when it comes to sex, we think prudence means prudish and is therefore uncool, and use prayer only when desperate about the repercussions from our impure immodesty.

Genetically and Environmentally Controlled Sibling Study. Developmental Psychology, May 08, 2017

What role models do our youngsters see in the culture? They observe pop stars and entertainers dress, speak, and behave in ways unrelated to any traditional moral code, and then see the resulting attention—or, adulation—showered upon them by the influential media and millions of adoring youngsters. When these people crash and burn, they are turned into heroes. The see seriously confused people who think their sex and gender from birth were wrong, and then are celebrated as heroic and courageous for publicly declaring that mismatch and then changing that creation. Those honorifics demonstrate the first sin of pride, with the creatures proclaiming they have become—or always were—the Creator. There are many things wrong with this new trend, one that seems to be the ultimate manifestation of radical freedom with people making themselves gods, therefore asserting they can do or become anything they want—regardless of the detachment from right reason, reality, truth and, yes, God.

Society has either redefined or rejected the concepts of sin, evil, moral, and normal. Since "it's all good" and "all relative," there can be "no worries" because each of us can define his or her own "normal," demanding that everyone label it thusly no matter how untrue it is and has been throughout human history. This change is "all about me" rather than "we" or "thee," and "me" expects to get whatever "me" wants. Adults, however, are supposed to be the leaders in a culture, so they bear the greatest responsibility.

Of the four cardinal virtues, prudence is the overarching one, as it indicates the practice of good judgment and restraint. Today, ironically, many would instead refer to those demonstrating this behavior as prudes, implying an unsophistication about things sexual. Something, however, changed over time, because the Old French and Latin roots of *prudence* show that it ultimately means, "intelligence, seeing ahead, practical knowledge and wisdom to see what is suitable or profitable."

Eros Love

Eros love is the chemistry that can bring us together. It can be the romantic love between a man and a woman that, as Pope Benedict XVI wrote in his first encyclical, *Deus Caritas Est* (God Is Love), "is neither planned nor willed, but somehow imposes itself upon human beings." The brief experience with Elvira aside, throughout my elementary school career there was little, if any, romantic love imposing itself on me, but that would soon change.

Upon graduation I expected to enter an all-boys Catholic high school. But my parents had different plans and instead sent me to a coed public school. Since this was 1970, the culture was very much in the throes of the hippie convulsion. One way this manifested itself was, once again, through the manner of girls' dress, or the lack thereof. It was a shock to me. Up to that time, modesty of dress by the girls in my life was the norm, either imposed by parents, clergy or religious sisters, or by the girls themselves, to control the imposition by eros, retain the virtue of chastity, and preserve and protect their dignity. That was evidence of the wisdom of prudence. And since people make up the culture, ours reflected such modesty. But the culture was changing, and distraction was a regular part of my school day. Many of the girls dressed in a way that little was left to wonder, thereby making me think I was falling in and out of eros several times a day during those years, something that couldn't have happened at the all-boys high school. And I believe this to be an example of the imposition to which Benedict was referring. But this chemistry does not keep us together. For a better understanding of this we must again turn to the ancient wisdom of Jews and Greeks as reference points in describing a fuller love.

Fulfilling Love

The Hebrew word for love is *Ahava*, in which "Hava" means *to give* and "ahav" means *complete devotion*, and this love is integral to the Jewish wedding ceremony. Additionally, *Chesed* represents for the Hebrews "loving kindness," or the covenant love of God for humanity. The Greek *"agape"* is a word Pope Benedict describes as a love that "involves a real discovery of the other, moving beyond the selfish. Love is no longer self-seeking in the intoxication of happiness (or madness); but instead seeks the good of the beloved…ready, and even willing, for sacrifice." This love is freely given. Not only can these loves not happen in pornography, but they also do not happen in too many of relationships today because our focus is on ourselves and only on what we can receive. Too many sons have faced the carnal temptress along their journeys, without ever having received the wise counsel necessary to reduce the risks of falling into the traps that have caught so many.

As a student of platonic philosophy, Augustine would have been knowledgeable about these loves, but he still struggled to become better. He wanted to focus on his education, as he "was roused to a desire for wisdom." But the pull of eros was strong, and he couldn't quite give up "this world's happiness, and all bodily pleasures." While praying for relief from his amorous desires, he wanted it done according to *his* timetable and not God's, leading to one of his most memorable prayers: "For I was afraid that You might quickly cure me of my dis-ease of lust before I have satisfied it." So the "dis-ease" of today is nothing new. But our social tumult is the result of a culture that misunderstands eros—and all the loves—therefore corrupting sex and gender.

In defining their masculinity, men throughout the world certainly emphasize sexuality, but according to surveys such as those published in the *Journal of Sexual Medicine* and *Journal of Men's Health* involving many thousands around the world, "being a man of honor" was ranked much higher than "having an active sex life." However, if an alien were to land near any movie theater, magazine rack, music recording studio, or in most TV and computer rooms in America, it would conclude that sexual activity of any kind—for pleasure absent conjugal unity and procreation—is our purpose. And using sex as a premise to sell throughout all media mostly involves the use of women's bodies.

For many, moving within and among this misunderstanding of romance can seem like moving among the flower garden, with the potential for many blooms and fragrances throughout the journey. We find, however, that some will be rosebushes and others stinging nettles, each with thorns whose pain lasts much longer than the blooms. These could be unwanted pregnancies, diseases, or broken trust. The big difference is that the plant's design, from which it cannot deviate, is only for defensive purposes, protecting the fragile beauty and fragrance of the flower. But men very often mistake these multiple relationship "blooms" as opportunities to manifest their poor understanding of manliness. Men *and* women mistakenly think of them as the romantic "falling in love," and represent the only kind of love. So when the raging passions ebb, as they must, we misinterpret the meaning and mistakenly end the relationship, proclaiming, in willful ignorance, our innocence because we've just "fallen out of love." When people conclude this during marriage, it is tragic because of the consequences.

By the time I was preparing for my marriage I was aware of only family love and romance, and had no sophistication about either. The first one just seemed to exist, absent any notion of feelings or effort other than, say, feeling protective of my younger sisters. Eventually I would learn the filial and agape loves and their purpose of giving rather than receiving, and learn that eros love is more complicated.

Many men believe manliness and achieving manhood are dependent upon or directly related to romantic relationships, and to what benefit they can receive rather than what good they can give. At the first ebb in feelings of romance, the relationships ultimately fade, and apart each goes in order to find the missing piece in someone else. But that piece could never be found because they didn't understand what it was that each of them was seeking. It wasn't until I was preparing for marriage that I found that piece: the agape love of making the *other person* primary and wanting to give to that person more than wanting to receive from her. The virtue potential within us is only actualized if we demonstrate more sensitivity, and makes the other person as important as we are.

I very much want all children, but especially boys, to understand that the greatest demonstration of manliness in love is giving love—in *all* its forms—to the other. That is true charity. Achieving excellence in the fullness of a man's journey—including his relationships—and then sharing that excellence with others to improve their lives is what makes him noble and heroic. It is not the "notches in his belt," nor, especially, how often he unbuckles that belt.

Very often people view waning passion as an alarm, warning that the relationship is in trouble and perhaps indicating that they were not meant for each other. Thinking this, many wonder how marriage can endure and if they should marry. Again, this betrays a misunderstanding of love and romance, focusing as it does on oneself rather than the other person in the relationship.

Unfortunately, my father and I never had any detailed talk about intimate relationships, but if he had brought up sex or romance, I'm not sure what my reaction would have been. However, I am fairly sure I would not have reacted in the same manner as my daughter initially did when, upon hearing from me that I wanted to talk with her about relationships, said, "I'm going to throw up," and then made a rescue telephone call to her brother! We did still have a conversation, however incomplete it was.

Upon realizing I had met my relational destiny with the woman who would become my wife, the engagement soon followed, with marriage six months away. In preparation for receiving the Catholic sacrament of matrimony, we were required to take a preparatory course known as "pre-Cana" (Cana is the village in the New Testament where Jesus attended a wedding and performed His first public miracle, or sign: turning water into wine).

I had expressed to our priest my strong resistance to this obligation, because in my ignorance and hubris I couldn't imagine what the church could tell me about love and marriage. Yet it turned out to be one of the greatest lessons of my life. The course described the emotional eros, but emphasized filial and agape: the committed and divine loves whose source founded the very church in which our vows would be spoken and consecrated. We were therefore taught that permanent love is a decision, a choice—an act of will—to commit to the love of the other regardless of the level of eros at any given moment during the marriage. This decision was to be based upon manageable reason rather than just the uncontrollable and unreliable flames of passion.

Deciding to love was a concept completely new to me. It meant that during times in which the surface water of my feelings of eros love would rise and fall with the waves of life, the deeper regions of my decision to show filial and agape love would remain constant and steady. This explanation was based upon St Paul's teaching that the summit of life is love. However, in that text the Greek word repeatedly used is not *feeling* love, but *doing* love—just as it is with the aforementioned *ahava*. It is always a verb, and therefore always an action *to do* for the benefit of the other. And we choose our actions, and can do so, independently of how we feel. Without action, how else would others know our love?

This lesson was driven home to me on the eve of one Saint Valentine's Day, many years into my marriage, as I struggled to decide if I should write a poem for my wife. I'd written many prior to this, and although all were motivated by eros, filial and agape loves, my feelings on this occasion were paramount. However during this situation, I was not *feeling* any love; rather, I was upset over some disagreement between us. I was in the realm of feelings—mostly mine—and therefore subject to their turbulent waters.

The children had gone to bed, and not long after them went my wife. And so I was left in my chair with pen and paper, as well as my churning thoughts and feelings that contrasted sharply with the quiet of night. As the lone lamp cast a soft glow in the immediate area of the otherwise darkened room, I distinctly recall feeling only a strong desire to leave the paper blank and dig deeper into my mental trench of being wronged. I looked out the windows to stare into the darkened neighborhood, but instead saw only my reflection in the glass. Yet something flashed in that reflection, and looking down I realized it was my wedding ring. Seeing this immediately brought me back to my pre-Cana lesson regarding the "decision to love." I also thought of Kevin and Maureen, and realized that were I to be selfish and go with my feelings at that moment, my actions could be a slippery slope toward further troubles.

And so I willed my love into action without feeling any, and began writing what has become one of my favorite poems. In it I describe the importance of this other love, by having "*decided* to wear the gold ring" because the marriage was not just about my feelings and me but also about the children, the truth of our union, and God. So the marital tempest passed as both filial and agape loves asserted their roles, encouraging eros to eventually return.

The experience proved to be a great lesson for me. We have the ability to control those unbidden feelings, however powerful they can be (as Augustine made clear), but we don't always have the will. It is my fervent hope that children learn this concept, because of its priceless and enduring value.

Disintegration of Our Nature

When the Food and Drug Administration approved Enovid, it proved to be a breakthrough for birth control and a signal of full freedom for eros—but not without a cost. The various pill contraceptives (abortifacients or not) that obstruct the natural order and function of our bodies have had significant indirect effects beyond their intended actions. The consequences of both have rippled and raged throughout much of our modern culture.

The pill has, generally, freed from worry those of us with concerns about pregnancy, and surveys show that most favor this way. But while it has allowed men and women to relate more freely at a biological level, it has made it easier for us to move farther apart on rational, emotional, and spiritual levels. Very often, commitment is not even a shadow in the room, let alone a presence. By the mid-1960s, our culture had become sexualized, and our accounting would come later.

In 1968, Pope Paul VI issued the encyclical *Humanae Vitae*, detailing the church's teaching on birth control. This document was partly based upon the "principle of totality" from Aristotle and Aquinas, teaching that the parts of one's body only have meaning when *integrated* and in relation to the good order of the body—as designed by God. It was a comprehensive expression of how marital love perfectly unites male and female in openness to the natural order of procreation and to the upbringing of that creation. The papal letter was also a warning, about how obstructing the natural order harms both the personal and social orders.

This encyclical was not, as is often portrayed, an announcement and explanation of a new commandment: "Thou shalt not enjoy sexual relations." However, it was, and continues to be, roundly criticized, mocked, and ignored by the culture, including those choosing to become "ex-Catholics" because of this decision. The critics wanted the church to stay out of the bedroom, if not everything else. But when one compares the predictions made in the encyclical to the cultural decline, the pope appears to have been prophetic. He warned of:

- Increased marital infidelity
- A general decline in moral standards
- A reduction in the reverence of women by men
- The potential for nations to set policy and force the limitation of family size

The pope was not alone in his warnings, and was, in fact, preceded decades earlier by Mohandas Gandhi who said, "As it is, man has sufficiently degraded her (women) for his lust; and artificial methods, no matter how well-meaning its advocates may be, will still further degrade her. Any large use of these methods is likely to result in the dissolution of the marriage bond and free love." Framing his message in love, Paul VI lamented the change and asked, "How can love deny the transmission of life?" The subsequent evidence may or may not show that the pill explicitly caused these changes in our moral behavior, but the correlation is quite strong.

Many would say there is nothing wrong with this new behavior, expressing the libertarian "live and let live;" but libertine conduct has resulted from this sexual liberty, thereby allowing, if not encouraging, behavior that has coincided with abortion, divorce, same-sex marriage and gender identity confusion. Modern birth control seems to have changed our identity from moral beings that strive for restraint, purity and dignity, to sexual beings of unrestrained self-expression. The principal relationship is family; and since the sexual revolution, the birth rate in the Western world has plummeted while divorce has skyrocketed.

The Break with Tradition

Virtue is manifest by behaving toward others with charity and integrity, and this is especially important in romance. But very often we are not so intentional, and become, therefore, less virtuous. While undignified behavior for many of us may have been long ago, the lessons of those experiences should be as recent as our memories and guide us throughout our lives. Yet the dissolution of so many marriages, including my own, suggests that for too many of us the commitment we proclaimed went no deeper than our vocal chords. As we maintain this superficiality, our hyper-sexualized culture continues with all its consequences. Family breakdown reflects a profound selfishness—exploring each other for the treasures that make "me" feel good, and when *those* treasures are no longer found there is little regard for the ramifications of our subsequent selfish actions. Thus we make ourselves complicit in the tragedy of our children's apathy, antipathy or fear about a covenantal relationship. Our behavior has failed to enlighten them about the great benefits of a virtuous life, and so they have become accustomed to the safe, single life, content with their designer coffee, skinny jeans, apps—and pets but no children. The desire for that covenantal life based upon morality, dignity and goodness, or the hope for it, has therefore lessened.

According to the Pew Research Center, the percentage of men and women aged 25 or older who have never married has more than doubled since 1960, and two-thirds of 18- to 29-year-olds believe society is just as well off if people have priorities other than marriage and children. The most common priorities seem to be money, career and comfort, all pointing to something deeper. And who can blame them? They have been taught (and scarred) by the self-centered behavior of their parents. Perhaps they are thinking that fewer babies mean less competition for their job as they age. If that is true, then let us hope the remaining one-third will have enough children to offset the barrenness of the others, so that sufficient numbers of scientists, entrepreneurs, philosophers and plumbers will be born to maintain some of what remains of this country's exceptionalism—after the two-thirds are gone!

A deeper examination of this new behavior pattern seems to uncover individualism and radical freedom, along with the aforementioned doubt. The Pew survey indicates at least two reasons for the lowered priority of marriage and family: fear of divorce (expressed by both sexes) and the difficulty women have reported in finding a "good" man (so much for "no-fault" divorce). What happened to men of good, just and moral character? The effects of technology, gender feminism, and the poor behavior of men seem to have decreased their presence and value, or at least the perception of that value.

An example of this attitude was highlighted in the popular 1990s television show *Murphy Brown*, a sitcom that revolved around the life of an unmarried female reporter. She was the prototype who demonstrated how liberated women could have it all—high-powered careers, sex on demand, and family—with little involvement from men. As the season progressed, she revealed her late-age pregnancy and that her boyfriend (not husband) did not want to trade his lifestyle for that of a family. She decided to have the baby. Her decision was celebrated, but not because she kept their baby rather than abort it. Instead, her pregnancy and single motherhood were celebrated as if the baby was some type of trophy and the mother could do it all without a father or husband.

A big reason this episode gathered so much attention was that it appeared during the presidential campaign, and Vice President Dan Quayle commented on it as part of a much larger speech on the moral decline in the culture and family. "It doesn't help matters," asserted Mr. Quayle, "when primetime TV has Murphy Brown, a character who supposedly epitomizes today's intelligent, highly paid professional woman, mocking the importance of fathers by bearing a child alone and calling it just another lifestyle choice."

The firestorm that followed from the media and feminists was not surprising, as "identity politics" was on an ascendant trajectory. The main reason was that the Vice President spoke the truth, one that many did not want to hear. He had touched a third rail in this country by expressing opposition to a "protected" group, something that is a no-no in politically correct America. Yet it was only a year later that *The Atlantic* magazine published an article titled "Dan Quayle Was Right" by Barbara Dafoe Whitehead. She wrote, "The social-science evidence is in: though it may benefit the adults involved, the dissolution of intact two-parent families is harmful to large numbers of children." A blurb accompanying the article notes, "Family diversity, in the form of increasing numbers of single-parent and stepparent families does not strengthen the social fabric but, rather, dramatically weakens and undermines society." And in the vast numbers of cases, a mother led the broken family, and father was no longer around.

Robert Rector, writing for the Heritage Foundation in 2012, gives further support to Ms. Whitehead and Mr. Quayle by showing that "marriage drops the probability of child poverty by 82%" and that "71% of poor families with children are not married." He goes on to assert, "The collapse of norms concerning marriage and having children has been a disaster." If the findings from this research raised any alarms, they didn't seem to register with the populace. Are we on the inevitable road to perdition?

CHAPTER 13

Have We Cause for Hope?

*It could only be a genuine regard for virtue that had
brought back the poor wanderer to its paths*
Hester Prynne *The Scarlet Letter*

NATHANIEL HAWTHORNE

WHEN A DEFENSE HOLDS FROM a courageous stand against a seemingly inevitable defeat, hope is the natural response. Not long ago, The Catholic University of America (CUA) took such a stand by returning to a policy of single-sex dormitories. The main reason for this change was the administration's effort to keep the college true to its full Catholic identity, which means adhering to traditional Catholic teaching on virtuous relationships in order to maintain the dignity of each person involved. Some of the Church's critics could argue that this same Church demonstrated little virtue during its recent sex scandals. That criticism would be fair, for a small percentage of its members. However, defenders of the Church should respond with three important points: 1) the disgraceful behavior of a small percentage does not negate the virtue of that Church or the truth of its teachings; 2) the Church has responded to its problem by becoming a role model for large organizations on how to properly and effectively address and prevent further abuse; 3) two of the Church's harshest critics—Hollywood and the media—are mired in their own sex scandals. These groups could learn from the Church; but their pride will prevent that corrective, allowing hypocrisy to continue.

As they have with other aspects of a child's education, parents should bear the primary responsibility for educating their children about good relationships. However, since many of us do not adequately fulfill that responsibility, schools have attempted to do that with a very broad brush. So what kind of education should we provide? The increasing problem of sexually transmitted diseases (STDs) in the early twentieth century prompted the beginning of sex education in the culture, informed by health, morality, and modesty. However, while the emphasis in prominent modern curricula still emphasizes health, both morality and modesty seemed to have been dropped from the curriculum. In their places have moved personal pleasure and the radical individual freedom to experience that pleasure, both informing the culture's new definitions of sex, gender and family but with an incomplete understanding of love, dignity and truth.

For example, in their *Guidelines for Comprehensive Sexuality Education*, the Sexuality Information and Education Council of the United States (SIECUS) offers this option during Level 1 instruction, to students ages 5 to 8:

- "Both boys and girls have body parts that feel good when touched."

Since "reproduction" is also mentioned in this level, it would have been more "comprehensive" to continue with "*and these parts were designed to help men and women make babies during marriage, and to help each couple enjoy a loving and committed relationship.*" In earlier eras, if public school students asked, "Who designed these lovely parts?" most teachers would have answered, "God," thereby placing the subject in a moral context but not necessarily a formal religious one. Yet with lawsuits such as *Elk Grove Unified School District v. Newdow*, one that challenges the recitation of the Pledge of Allegiance because it includes the words "under God," that answer is impossible to imagine.

The SIECUS educational curriculum also presented lessons on same-sex attraction and gender identity as variants on the normative sex and gender spectrums, as have increasing numbers of public school systems. These examples point to the great progress made by proponents since the public outcry in the 1990s against books such as *Heather Has Two Mommies*.

The philosophy behind these efforts has been rapidly affirmed with the help of various legal decisions, most notably that of *Obergefell v. Hodges* by the Supreme Court, and despite growing opposition by those who assert that a highly controversial agenda was being forced upon society without sufficient research to support it. Some of the leverage used by supporters of same-sex marriage included the assertion that children of parents with SSA fared at least as well as children living with their biological mother and father. This belief is behind the "no differences" theory, one that the American Psychological Association affirmed in 2004 but which would be challenged by further scientific scrutiny.

In 2012, Mark Regnerus, sociologist from the University of Texas (UT), published his landmark research entitled "How different are the children of parents who have same-sex relationships? Findings from the New Family Structures Study (NFSS)." The results showed that children raised by parents with SSA fared significantly worse than did children brought up in a traditional family in areas such as educational attainment, gender identity, sexual activity behavior, employment, academic and mental health. Not surprisingly, the publication of this research brought upon Dr. Regnerus a firestorm of protest and objection by proponents of the new "family," some of it personal, causing UT to open an inquiry into the possibility of scientific misconduct. They didn't find any. Instead, their thorough analysis reaffirmed the results.

In 2016, Donald Paul Sullins, professor of sociology at The Catholic University of America, published studies whose results seem to buttress the results of Regnerus; they showed that children of same-sex parents and children of same-sex *married* parents are much more likely to develop a variety of psychological and developmental problems than are children of opposite-sex parents.

Another indication of the philosophy behind the SIECUS guidelines as they relate to sex and gender is contrasted by the Level 3 guidelines (ages 12 to 15) for "body image" and "gender identity." *Body Image* guidelines indicate:

- "Some people may develop *disordered* eating as a result of how they feel about their bodies." (Emphasis added)

Considering the high rates of depression, suicide attempts and actual suicides, it was right to label this mind-body problem as a *disorder*, but it would have been better to add a message about the importance of getting help so as to restore order. Yet when we look at the guidelines for Gender Identity, no reference is made to anything being disordered. The answer seems to be, perhaps unintentionally, within the guidelines themselves. In its explanation of "transgender," SIECUS includes the following:

- "'Transgender' describes people whose internal sense of gender (gender identity) doesn't match what *society* expects of them based on their genitals and chromosomes (biological sex). (Emphasis added)

In other words, the problem for those identifying as being the sex opposite of their birth reality is not their own disorder, but rather *society's disordered expectation* of a male being male and female being female.

This absence is striking for a number of reasons, the first being the explicit lack of order between what the person believes and what that person would see either while standing naked in front of a mirror or while looking through an electron microscope at a DNA tissue sample. Another reason to indicate a disorder is expressed in those very same guidelines, which indicate the need for hotlines, support services and medical/surgical intervention to "re-order" the perceived self-description. Finally, depression and suicide rates for the transgender population are markedly greater than the rate for those with eating disorders. It is fair to opine and perhaps assert that some of these higher rates are due to the understandably difficult life of one identifying as transgender. With all these data pointing to a disorder, why would the guidelines not include it?

Thinking back to my ninth grade sex ed class with Mr. D, I recall him restoring order after our juvenile minds caused our immature reaction to his anatomy "art," and then, in his booming voice, launching into an explanation that the purpose of these parts was for reproduction, however pleasant the mechanics for that process. He then described some of the problems we'd likely find if these and other parts went uncontrolled during romance: "Boys, if you allow *down below* to do the thinking for *up above*, then you better be prepared for five minutes of heaven followed by the rest of your life in hell!"

At the time, Mr. D was referring to unwanted pregnancies, syphilis and gonorrhea, but he could not have known the terrible scourges and upheaval that would emerge over the next forty years, afflictions that resulted from the thinking that confused the pleasure of anatomy with its purpose—the very reason the sexual anatomy and activity exists. But today, if Mr. D tried offering help to youngsters troubled or confused about their sexuality or, especially, gender, then he could be branded a lawbreaker and pilloried as a bigot and hater. Those who knew him and his bighearted nature would have no trouble countering that branding.

In the spring 2017 issue of *The New Atlantis*, public health researchers lay out a case for putting the breaks on this runaway train. In their report, "Growing Pains: Problems With Puberty Suppression in Treating Gender Dysphoria," Paul W. Hruz, Lawrence S. Mayer and Paul R. McHugh urge caution about the rush to embrace the "affirmative" treatment model for this illness in children, since puberty-suppressing drugs and affirmative psychotherapy—to say nothing of surgery—are experimental and potentially harmful and irreversible.

A position statement made by the American College of Pediatricians in May 2017 supports these warnings, noting, "According to the DSM-V (Diagnostic and Statistical Manual of Mental Disorders-5th edition), as many as 98% of gender confused boys and 88% of gender confused girls eventually accept their biological sex after naturally passing through puberty." Knowing that the probability of suicide in those having had sex reassignment surgery is at least 19 times more likely than average, urging caution—if not cessation—would seem to make sense. Otherwise, the treatment smacks of child abuse.

Masculine Gender and Manhood

Traditions about gender formation were born from our biology and fully formed over eons from our natural environment. Historical and anthropological data, such as that detailed by David D. Gilmore in *Manhood in the Making: Cultural Concepts of Masculinity*, show that the vast majority of cultures valued manhood, and defined it in similar ways. Gilmore identifies "parallels of male imagery around the world" and "the approved way of being an adult male in any given society" so that society can be orderly and cohesive.

Gilmore and other researchers (Lonner, Archer, and Lloyd, et al.) found "striking regularities in standard male and female roles across cultural boundaries." They regularly found that males had to pass arduous tests to move from maleness to manhood and thereby distinguish anatomy from a societal recognition of the moral, prudent and temperate use of that anatomy. Could these be the tests to which Joseph Campbell refers along the hero's journey? If the boys failed them, then their lack of manliness was identified publicly by ridicule. When boys and men, in our culture and others, fail to meet the presumptive definition of manliness, they suffer rebuke that could include the slurs of "unmanly" and "effeminate," or hear the derisive taunts to "act like a man!" It seems reasonable to consider that this ridicule, and the stigma that occurs in our own culture, contributes to the aforementioned psychological and medical problems. Harsh though they were, it was the norm. One wonders why the author found the regularity of male roles striking, since history shows masculinity has been a natural outgrowth of maleness in virtually all cultures. But if you're from any number of colleges or universities, gender norms do not exist.

For many, that definition implies a machismo reliant on physical prowess. And while not every adult female was considered a lady, there was little uncertainty that each was a woman, for it was not her gender that was questioned as much as it was her lack of social refinement, personal integrity and, perhaps, dignified femininity.

While cultures existed that allowed androgyny, this was by far the great exception. And that rare individual still had to adhere to the cultural norms associated with whichever gender they ultimately chose. Gender formation toward masculinity for men and femininity for women was intentional by those who helped form the members of these cultures, simply as a natural progression of the spontaneous norms from childhood. While this formation pattern has been historically true, social engineers in North America have been working diligently over recent decades to dramatically change it.

I have compassion for those suffering from all this confusion, as I believe their pain is real. However, suffering urges upon us a corrective treatment, which would seem to be the humane response to the problem rather than affirmation that allows the disorder to deepen—especially in children whose brains are not fully formed. It would also be one that is most aligned with the correct understanding of our freedom to know the truth that many believe is revealed in the Biblical story of Creation.

Writing in his first encyclical as pope, John Paul II's *Redemptor Hominis* (The Redeemer of Man) ties freedom inextricably to truth: "For freedom on the one hand is for the sake of truth, and on the other hand it cannot be perfected except by means of truth. Hence, the words of our Lord, which speak so clearly to everyone: 'The truth will make you free' (John 8:32). *There is no freedom without truth*" (Emphasis added). But if truth and morality are subjective, in the relativism discussed elsewhere in this book, then each person can make his or her own imagined reality—an oxymoron at best and a serious disorder at worst. And if enough people believe this way, then social policies that were historically based upon truth are rejected, and replaced by those whose foundation is false. Christian charity does not accompany people while encouraging them to do a wrong, even if that is what they express a desire to do; rather, it is to guide them to the true purpose of their existence.

The Process of Learning

While writing this book, I have principally striven to keep children's formation in mind. The sins of my distant past felled me along my hero's journey, but only temporarily. Personal reflection can help us learn from our errors of judgment, and God's grace can help us restore a good conscience and resume traveling our heroic path.

The direction our culture has taken disturbs me. I believe Western Civilization is becoming less civilized, and is in a rapid decline. It is heading in the wrong direction, one that is not heroic and one that will therefore increase the confused wanderings of our children—especially our boys. Some who disagree will label me as intolerant or worse, and then demonstrate hypocrisy by being harshly intolerant and hateful to me. Harshness and hatred are on the rise, but an opposition seems to be forming.

When men fail to act heroically and reject the ancient truths of justice, morality, goodness and wisdom, then the resultant suffering should be the forge that transforms us into better versions of ourselves. Those men who believe in the truth of this message—and there are many—must exhort each other to lovingly affirm the dignity and masculinity of the young men in our lives; encourage them to moral virtue; help them find the purpose of their existence; and, teach them that dignified behavior reinforces their dignity. Boys must know that their self-worth can only be found by honorably striving for excellence in the fulfillment of that purpose, and to help others do the same. The example of those who transform their suffering into a life of honor and decency is crucial to those who can learn from them; and while the greatest representative of this virtue is called "Son of God," the moral behavior of mere mortals also becomes the basis for our hope in what it means to be called a "man."

Without minimizing the suffering of anyone going through any particular struggle, Thomas More believed each of us could unfold a greater meaning from the circumstances and always find what he called a "medicinal" benefit from them. He wasn't referring specifically to health, but in the context of the great spiritual struggles of his time. This greater meaning came from a better use of one's mind, will and faith. Whether the conviction of his beliefs, and the heroic actions wrought from them, were in part due to his personality, I cannot say, but the fortitude and loyalty he demonstrated from a well-formed conscience despite the looming threat from his king, strongly indicate something more.

CHAPTER 14

Faith from Our Father, and His Son

The ordinary arts we practice every day at home are of more importance to the soul than their simplicity might suggest.

—Thomas More

Ecce Homo

—Pontius Pilate

For years during Kevin's childhood and adolescence, I would bring him with me into New York City, sometimes to work for me but mostly to have fun. On one particular day in the summer of 2005, we were enjoying a stroll up Fifth Avenue, on our way to visit Saint Patrick's Cathedral. We soon saw the great spires of that majestic edifice, but almost immediately my attention was drawn to a solitary cloud, one that seemed to move right over the building. There was some irony in that cloud, because it struck me as representative of shadows over too many churches during that period, each a symbol of the horrible sex scandal involving some of the clergy and the youth under their care. The dark shadow from this particular cloud seemed to loom larger as we drew nearer, because at the time, Saint Patrick's was itself mired in a scandal.

It is almost as difficult for me to experience and explore problems in my church, as it would be for me to do the same with my children. The main reason is my love for and devotion to it. Secondarily is the frustration knowing the smug satisfaction felt by a culture that is increasingly antagonistic to Christianity—especially Catholicism—and whose hypocrisy is made clear by its own celebration of sexuality unhinged to any traditional morality, simultaneously condemning both the moral stance of the church as well as its sins. And speaking of sin, another great irony is that this same culture denies even the *existence* of sin—at least in itself. One does not minimize the problem by asserting the truth that the rate of religious sex scandals is similar to or less than those in many other fields. But since no other group acts *in persona Christi*, a higher standard is implied—and rightly so. Therefore, explore we must in order to know the truth, expunge the evil and heal the sickness—in our loved ones, our church, and ourselves.

At the time of this trip, that dark cloud involved the rector of the cathedral we were about to enter, a scandal that was all over the news. But unlike the predominantly homosexual nature of the church scandals, especially those involving children, this one reportedly involved a heterosexual relationship that the monsignor adamantly denied until his death. Thinking that Kevin, in his early teens at the time, may have heard about this case, I made sure we talked about the problem. During the conversation, I pointed toward the cathedral and said, "The scandals are not the faith. Sins from those within the church may challenge one's faith or, better yet, one's belief in that church, and we should cry out for justice in defense of those who have been victimized, but those sins do not represent the faith. That would be tantamount to me rejecting the aspirational truths penned in our nation's founding documents, because of the wrong acts of our politicians." So, why should Kevin and Maureen persevere in their belief? And what is this faith of Christianity, in which their trust rests?

As it is with most children, mine experienced religion in its joyful, solemn and mysterious rituals, as a continuation of family tradition in which they perceived an importance with only a basic understanding. Their experience is no doubt typical, considering the profound nature of Catholicism and some of its complex doctrines. In line with that tradition, the acceptance of a faith relationship by children is more likely when they have a loving relationship with their parents, and when their parents model for them a loving relationship with their faith.

Whether children or adult, true faith relationships are formed by encounters with those whose hearts and motives we believe can be trusted, and become deepened as that trust manifests itself in acts of good will. The doctrines I mentioned, when properly explained, do not spark the relationships but instead help them grow deeper. Rituals must have an element of the mysterious; but they become illuminated when built upon the concept of *anamnesis*, which is a *lived remembrance* of past sacred events in which we *enter into* their holiness. We are not casual bystanders. The best example of this for all Catholics and many Christians is our remembrance of the Last Supper, which is the final meal shared by Jesus and his Apostles before his death. In the celebration of Holy Eucharist, or sacred thanksgiving, we give glory to God for all the good of creation—including our existence and the great potential resulting from it. But in recent decades, the communal and relational aspects have retreated and allowed a distant creedal faith to assume prominence. This change is far from the intent of its founder, and one that has prompted many to leave the church.

When I have had discussions with "former Catholics" about the reasons they left the church, many cited a bad personal experience as the prominent cause of the damaged relationship, while others complained of getting nothing out of worship and having no relationship. While the interpretation of these bad experiences may or may not have been incorrect, the manner in which the *institutional* church behaved during those experiences or in its response has often been insensitive at best. Other respondents indicated that they did not feel welcome, a problem that would seem to be easy to resolve but one that, unfortunately, still persists. My initial reaction to the first two reasons was to become defensive about the church, as if I were defending a family member (which, in a way, I was). But I quickly learned that that was a failing strategy, if their reasons were legitimate and if my goal was to have them "come home." I came to believe that each response held at least some truth, and that I should respect it and be charitable toward it. The next step would be to explore a better way that might encourage them, to move beyond those bad experiences and help them to *want* to return in order to share faith *relationships* with like-minded believers.

The most common reason I hear—"I wasn't getting anything out of it"—indicates a profound misunderstanding about the purpose of our religious tradition and its rituals. It is similar to the confusion about love that we discussed earlier, in that those giving this response think the ceremonies revolve around *them* and that *they* are to be satisfied. That emphasis on oneself creates a passive mindset of one waiting to *only* receive a benefit rather than stressing the importance of us actively giving and sharing in the sacred experience of *remembrance*. However I believe that the underlying reason for all these replies is the emptiness of their experience, due to the absence of any *relationship* within their faith, and all that it represents.

Throughout the millennia of the Christian tradition, faith formation has been a significant factor in the development of a child's identity. His sense of well-being and self-worth were based largely on the belief that his birthright, or inheritance, was in being a special creation of a loving Creator. Not long ago a tradesman was at my house, and as part of a broader conversation about raising children he commented, "Religion is ok if it makes weak people feel better," implying that faith is the "opiate" of Karl Marx or a 911 call to God for those of us lacking the strength to handle a crisis. But how does he even know about God, let along religion? He doesn't realize that his awareness of a Creator came from someone who had learned from someone else who had learned…and on and on throughout millennia and across cultures back to the beginning.

What is the basis for this universally held desire for meaning, purpose and something more ("the Big *More*, or transcendence," as explained by Dr. Gower, theologian and professor at Georgian Court University). Is this transcendent *more*, something or someone that exists only beyond our world, to which we might escape? Or, is it both within and beyond, helping each of us to know that we are more than our current understanding of ourselves, and that we can see a greater meaning in all our experiences? Does not the ever-present desire for transcendence imply the existence of transcendence? It would seem so. But wrestling over *transcendence* is not going to encourage my tradesman to believe, nor bring people into a community of believers. There must be something more.

For two millennia, countless people have found that something—or rather someone—in Jesus of Nazareth. The first of these people were Jesus' contemporaries, during the three years of his public ministry, and their encounter with him began with an *invitation*—either from him or from one disciple to others. That should be a lesson for all of us; because from that simple gesture of kindness and the love that was behind it, sprang the greatest movement and force for good in history. And this unbound love made a trusting relationship possible, despite many presumed barriers.

One of the greatest examples to illustrate this trust, and the transcendent "More" described above, is found in the meeting between Jesus and the Samaritan woman at the well. In this gospel narrative by John we find Jesus transcending a number of cultural proscriptions, including those against Jews interacting with Samaritans let alone a Jewish *man* relating with an *unmarried* Samaritan *women* who has had five husbands. Whether or not these serial marriages reflected poorly on her choices or on the choices of men who may have abused her, we do not know. But we can infer from this story that she must have been at the peripheries of society, because women typically had younger female helpers to draw water and would gather in groups at the well during the cooler evening hours. So this profile suggests she probably had few if any trusting relationships and was alienated from much of the community. Knowing this, Jesus wanted to offer a relationship with her, one far better than those suggested in their exchange and one that would help her transcend her current limitations. This could only happen if she believed she could trust him, and his claim that, "whoever drinks the water I give them, will never thirst." Her subsequent evangelization, within her own Samaritan community, was testimony of having found that trust.

This relationship is deepened by the belief that our Creator is revealed in the Nazarene who says, "If you have seen me, you have seen the Father." And the systematic process, by which we can know about, form and grow this relationship, is called "Religion." This system helps us experience the sacred, by teaching us that our existence is a gift from that loving Creator and that we can flourish and ultimately be fulfilled by engaging lovingly with him and his creation. For Christians, that encounter is fostered by the belief that our Creator revealed himself to us, ultimately by becoming human.

As Augustine and others understood from the Latin root of "religion," *relegare*, the faith that we practice and beliefs we hold helps us "to bind fast with God." As each of us makes this faith pilgrimage, we increasingly understand the sacredness of all his creation and the love that binds us to each other and, ultimately, to him. Since this love is only manifest in our actions with others, faith teaches us to engage with people as a community of believers along that same journey, sharing the expressions of this relational faith and forming charitable practices that then become its traditions, all in an effort to return that community to its Creator. We move closer to this "union" by continuously giving witness to it, in our loving acts of service that culminate in the final step of our heroic journey. The urge for that union is beautifully described by Augustine, when he confesses that, "You have made us for yourselves, O Lord, and our hearts are restless until they rest in thee." That is our tradition, one ancient and cross-cultural.

Since the source of our faith is also the source of our being—our essence—faith cannot be a *thing* "out there" that we occasionally put on like we do nice clothing during Christmas, Easter or Passover, or something we reach for only in response to emergencies. After his dramatic conversion experience, the apostle Paul turned away from his persecution of Christians and toward the formation of them, building faithful communities through preaching, teaching and writing. In one of his letters to believers within the city of Corinth, written just two decades after Jesus' crucifixion, he exhorted them to understand the sacredness of their existence and the faith that springs from it, saying, "Do you not know that your body is a temple of the Holy Spirit, who is in you, whom you have received from God?" The religious system behind Christianity informs us about our inherent holiness, and encourages us to be holier—not than thou but than we were, and to not live a random life but one of purpose that leads to a fulfilling and glorious end.

For many adults, faith requires consent based upon a trust in the information and, most especially, the person providing that information—without going any deeper. For others, this belief is the basis from which they gain greater knowledge in order to grow into a fuller understanding of it, echoing Saint Anselm's motto, "Faith seeking understanding." And so we must seek a greater faith rather than wait passively for the bolt from heaven, and that involves further inquiry, spiritual practices and works of mercy.

What Has Become of That Tradition?

Surveys by groups such as Gallup and Pew Research Center indicate that today's adults—men in particular—have removed themselves from this engagement and the corresponding role because they have removed themselves from church or any religious practice—if not from faith altogether. The impact on their children—and the culture—has been significant, evidenced by the dramatic decline in the younger generation's belief in God and with a corresponding rise in isolation and alienation. The results of this can be observed on any given Sunday in church, as women far outnumber men and young families are often unaccompanied by a father. What is the result of this absence?

In Pew's 2014 "Religious Landscape Study," 70% of those older than 65 professed a certainty about God while only 50% of adults under 30 did. One might conclude that the disparity simply reflects a firmer belief by those who are a lot nearer to meeting their maker. However, other data should make us reject that. The study also found that only 57% of men reported a degree of certainty about God, while almost 70% of women did. Perhaps that is the reason far more women than men involve themselves with church. Also noteworthy is that these figures represent a significant drop since 2007, and point to changes that are particularly true for the millennial generation. This group has grown up alongside rapid advances in science and technology, including artificial intelligence, and absent the ancient tradition in which both faith and reason provide the answers to the great questions of life. Finally, the percentage of those not believing in God has increased significantly in recent years. Maybe the data from a decade and before can help explain these changes. If a tradition is no longer taught, then its perceived value plummets—even if it purports to carry a powerful truth.

In the report, "The Demographic Characteristics of the Linguistic and Religious Groups in Switzerland," investigators Werner Haug and Phillipe Warner of the Federal Statistical Office found that a father's faith practice will very likely have a dramatic effect on the faith practiced by his children. Their research showed:

- Regular church attendance by both parents will result in 33% of their children being regular churchgoers and 41% being irregular. The balance of 26% will be lost.
- If dad infrequently attends church but mom regularly does, only 3 percent of their children will be regular practitioners of the faith while 59% will be irregular. In this scenario, 38% will be lost.
- If dad does not practice the faith but mom regularly does, only 2 percent of their children will worship faithfully and 37% occasionally. In this situation, the church loses *more than sixty percent* (emphasis added).

The above study is certainly not the final word, in part because of its limitations and partly because it doesn't help us much with the reason for the results. As much as I do not like seeing only women accompanying children into church and along the faith journey, I am grateful to all of them for engaging in that effort. There are many wonderful women bearing the burden of keeping faith alive in the family, a burden made heavier by the example of daddy's non-participation. The limitations of this research notwithstanding, it strongly implies a reality that the faith practice of a boy's father, while never guaranteeing faithful practice by that boy, impacts him significantly more than the same practice of his mother. Augustine's experience seems to be echoed in the aforementioned study, as we find this borne out in one of his struggles about his waning faith during his childhood: "I then already believed: and my mother, and the whole household, *except my father* (emphasis added): yet did not he prevail over the power of my mother's piety in me, that as he did not yet believe, so neither should I." (It is our great good fortune that his mother ultimately prevailed, but only after persistent prayer and many years.) And so follows the massive decline in the practice of Christianity, followed by the fading belief, and ultimately the free will rejection of faith. It is tempting to cast blame on the men for this problem, but that would only drive them further away. Instead it would be better to learn the reasons for their departure, and then work to accompany them back to their faith, their church and a personal encounter with Jesus Christ.

If, in a different scenario, a child's family lovingly exemplifies its religious faith as the children grow into adulthood, then an ongoing commitment will be more likely. This formation should help them respond better to their experiences of suffering, and to the threats leveled against them and their faith from the culture. In this way, they will be more likely to carry on the tradition to the next generation. This understanding affects our experience of joy and, especially, sorrow, because sorrow is the great equalizer among mankind and a great source of transformative power. Greater knowledge is especially important in a culture such as ours that is hostile to faith generally and to Christianity in particular, in order to effectively respond to those who think our modern sophistication has made religion an anachronism.

Some of the faithful grow up with a "peasant faith," believing as children do but without much understanding. In their charity, they give powerful witness to the faith and a reason to believe. We might consider some of Jesus' early disciples in this light. "Christianity" had yet to begin, and in its seminal stage was known simply as *The Way*; and those disciples no doubt needed to frequently remember their Lord, in order to remain on the right path. Those who believe but do not remember or practice, often lack conviction to the faith and any commitment. We should not look to this last group to teach and pass on the tradition, because they would eventually not be able to give a rationale for believing and perhaps no witness.

Many reject any faith as is commonly understood, replacing it with any number of "religions" such as health, sports, money or sex. Or they become a "None" as have so many Millennials: one having no religious affiliation. They might use the common phrase, "I'm spiritual, but not religious," to de-emphasize or dismiss the latter without the ability to explain the former and how it is a definite part of their lives. This Millennial "religion" has been labeled "Moralistic Therapeutic Deism" by sociologist Christian Smith, in his book *Soul Searching: The Religious and Spiritual Lives of American Teenagers*. The central goal of life for adherents to this morality, notes the author, is to be happy and to feel good about oneself; and the effort to realize this goal could involve either social justice actions, or actions that are more self-directed in order to engender those good feelings. One of the key points raised by the authors is how illiterate the teenagers are about faith and religious matters, and how important it is for them to be properly taught about these subjects.

This vague notion of spirituality contrasts sharply with the hard reality expressed by writers of many Christian texts, ancient and modern. Those writings frequently use the word *concrete* to make clear the definite nature of their faith and the saving actions of its founder, in contrast with some nebulous spirit onto which *Nones* could neither hold nor rely. In light of earlier references to my elementary school, it seems that as the number and influence of *nuns* has decreased, the number of *Nones* has increased.

Many *Nones* are spiritual "seekers" who search for the meaning and purpose in their lives, discoveries that all probably want but are either innocently or willfully ignorant of seeking. In all likelihood, those in this group sense something is missing in their lives, and the search begins. That search suggests the potential for an "implicit faith," observes Tomáš Halík, Catholic priest and author of *Night Of The Confessor*, in that people demonstrate behavior and values "fundamental to an attitude of faith." This does not only mean social justice actions, absent any private morality, but rather both.

We should hope that *Nones* who feel a sense of emptiness receive the spiritual direction similar to that which Augustine received, during his time under the mentorship of Ambrose, and learn about the complementarity of faith and reason. But unlike most throughout the last few millennia who believed the answers came from the intelligent and, perhaps, loving source of all existence, many today are trapped in the dark ignorance of their own cave and mistakenly direct their search at a different source for the sunlight of reason: Siri or Google.

But adherents to religious traditions must not condemn or disparage those who have walked away from those rituals. According to Father Halík, these "crises of religion...are enormous windows of opportunity opened to us by God. These are challenges for us 'to put out into the deep.'" We should explore reasons for this departure, and be the charitable witnesses modeled after the Good Samaritan that encourage more seekers to this faith. When Jesus related this parable to his disciples, its great meaning emerged. Rather than upbraid one with different beliefs by quoting Mosaic Law or Sabbath regulations, one stranger took pity on another and cared for his wounds. When Jesus' followers correctly answered his query as to the moral of the story, he simply said, "Go and do likewise."

God is Justice...

This Love, however, is also Truth and Justice, qualities of God that are increasingly minimized or rejected by those who simultaneously reject the realities of evil and sin, and therefore any consequences. These same people see Jesus as only loving, kind and tolerant, but never righteous, judgmental, or, worse, condemning. They believe, as suggested by theologian H. Richard Niebuhr, in a "God without wrath who brought men without sin into a kingdom without judgment through the ministrations of a Christ without a cross." They ignore the fact that in the first three Gospels, the first word of Jesus's public ministry was "Repent;" or they disregard his consistency in condemning evil, and its manifestation we call "Sin," while still offering forgiveness to all who turned away from their sin.

They forget that the one reason we were visited by the source of love, truth and justice was to save us from ourselves and lead us back to that source: God. And they don't understand that the discipline of justice causes the restoration of natural order. Parents should be truthful and just with their children, because they love them. But more remains to be done.

The God of Reason, and Much More...

Unlike any other creation, humans are rational, moral and self-conscious creatures. We have used this reason, this native intelligence, to emerge from the cave and explore ourselves, our world, and beyond. And during our explorations, we have searched for those answers. Our power of reason gave rise to the philosophical discipline, defined as the "love of wisdom," and its logic greatly helped us in that search—and always will. Aspects of the Catholic faith, for example, were greatly informed by the teachings of Plato and, especially, Aristotle. Philosophy and its logic inform our thinking about God and his revealed truths, and can be the vehicle that transports our understanding to great depths. Plato's highest Good illuminates the truth as the sun brings to light the reality that surrounds us. But is there more? As great as philosophy is, we found it could bring us only so far because of its reliance on the inherent limitations of our senses and reason. But what is the transcendent source of this reason? Unlike the rest of, say, instinctual creation, humans *chose* to believe there had to be more, using our will to move us further when reason had reached its limit. This transcendence is implied in a gentle caution by Dickens' Pickwick, "Such are the narrow views of those philosophers who, content with examining the things that lie before them, look not to the truths which are hidden beyond."

Religious experience, based upon both the rational and imaginative mind, binds us back to our origins and to the answers that go back to that beginning, helping us to untie our dilemma and enabling God's creatures to imagine the bond with their Creator in this life *and beyond*. So how did this bond come about?

The Jewish and Christian traditions gives us a comprehensive record of humanity's faith encounter of and relationship with its Creator, in His revealed gift of Himself into history as evidenced by the Hebrew patriarchs and prophets, followed by the birth of the Creator into the world of His creatures and the fulfillment of this tradition by His followers. Christianity is therefore an *historical* religious tradition; and is one based upon both faith and events in order to help move us forward *in time* from our origin to our destination, or "destinacionem," the Latin for "purpose or design"—in other words, our transcendent destiny. But unlike the imprisoning path of Melville's Captain Ahab, whose "path to my fixed purpose (the whale) is laid with iron rails, whereon my soul is grooved to run," the Christian's awe-filled freedom along the way to salvation offers his soul countless choices to leave the path—and return to it.

However while the traditions passed down are historical, faith is based upon much more than history. The basis for having faith in these traditions and being faithful from them, results from one's intellect and emotion, as well as imagination and will. The *intellect* uncovers logic in the faith legacy; the *emotional* aspect results from endearing experiences of another believer's charitable witness; the *imagination* finds the tradition attractive because of the larger reality to which its meta-physical and meta-historical mysteries point (e.g., "Transubstantiation": bread becoming the Body of Christ, and, Christ's resurrection); and then the *will* chooses. As Saint Paul said in his second letter to those in the church in Corinth who were struggling with false prophets, "So we fix our eyes not on what is seen, but on what is unseen, since what is seen is temporary, but what is unseen is eternal." Paul was a highly intelligent Pharisee, and therefore prone to neither shallow thinking nor flights of whimsy.

In this age of scientific materialism, faith is seen as simply the fiction of myth and is therefore rejected. But that rejection is unfortunate, as it is an uninformed decision. "Myths," notes Mary Lefkowitz, Classics scholar and expert in Greco-Roman history, "are stories with a religious content: they explain our relationship to forces beyond our control." Myths may have imagined characters, events and narratives, but the stories they tell relate to the reality of human experiences. Myths are like metaphors ("I'm as hungry as a horse") in that they contain truth and an imaginative fiction to help us unfold that truth. This is markedly different from an exclusive myth tradition that, however important to a culture, does not contain any historical reality or aspect of truth. They don't move with people through time to fulfill a destiny. And since they are not based upon truth, they are not dependent upon it.

As we strive to move forward in our faith decision we are greatly helped by, for example, the historical documents and archeological artifacts that at least give reasonable affirmation and at times confirmation of many biblical passages, and by the writings and works of the many brilliant faithful men and women who have built—and build upon—this tradition. As if forecasting Anselm's need for the believer to seek greater understanding," Augustine said, "We believe in order that we might understand. We understand in order that we might believe." Certainty would preclude the need for faith indicated by the Apostle Paul in his letter to the Hebrews, a correspondence that seeks to encourage the believers of a fledgling Christian community: "Faith is the realization of what is hoped for and evidence of things not seen." The things not seen hint at the intelligent mystery we may not yet be able to know, but can perceive. And saying "mystery" is not a copout. As Catholic theologian Frank Sheed said, *mystery* "does not mean a truth that we cannot know anything about, but a truth that we cannot know everything about."

Ultimately, believing Christians have a relationship with Jesus Christ through their trust in the Gospels, one that forms a bond and one that is largely the result of our free-will acceptance of the his divine gifts—especially his loving actions. That acceptance is faith. Not living in the time of the Messiah, we believe because of confidence in our faithful ancestors. We have that confidence because of Christ's response to the apostle Thomas in the Gospel of John, after our saint expressed disbelief in his fellow disciples' report of having seen the risen Lord, "You believe because you have seen. Blessed are those who haven't seen, but believe." As with any true gift, the love we encounter behind it is the most enduring and most meaningful part. The beliefs that express this faith are the living practices that attest to its merits. And "witness" is the key. But to what or, better yet, to whom do we give our witness?

Wager on Faith…

Faith presumes there is something more than that which we can know, or even perceive, and religious faith believes that natural life is neither the sum of our existence nor the purpose of our being. The faith of Christians is belief that the saving visit by their Creator to his troubled children was to transform us—by his love—and make sure we knew we had the opportunity to end up with him. That is the truism for those who believe. But what of those who choose not to believe, or those wanting to believe but who must first be certain? When Kevin and Maureen interact with agnostics and atheists, as each increasingly will, they might do well to keep in mind the gambling game of a French philosopher and mathematician.

In the history of Western philosophy, the 17th century Age of Reason was a period during which many believed all knowledge was learned solely by the power of our rational mind or from experience. Matters of faith, particularly the belief in God, were widely challenged, and one response supporting that belief came from Blaise Pascal, no intellectual slouch he.

Essentially, "Pascal's Wager" presents a game of logic, whose premise is that God does or does not exist, and you wager your life to believe or not believe in his existence, with the potential prize being your eternal happiness. You must bet on one or the other premise (theist or atheist) because we are in time and therefore have a destiny. In philosopher Peter Kreeft's wonderful explanation of this wager, being agnostic is impossible because we are not outside observers of life but participants in it. He notes that each of us is a ship on the waters of life with a limited supply of fuel, and as we move there is a port of eternal happiness, called "God." That sign, however, is not clear because of the fog of our unknowing, and the agnostic won't come in to port until he can be sure. But he will never be sure because our limitations mean that the fog will never clear, and he cannot remain at sea because the fuel will run out. As Kreeft puts it, "The Wager works because of the fact of death." In effect, not choosing becomes a default choice: atheism.

What it comes down to is this: if God does not exist, then it does not matter what you wagered (believed) because this life is all there is. Of course, you could still choose to live a good life. If, however, God exists, then your wager will determine your destiny after death. If at the end you chose not to believe, and lived a selfish life, then the existence of God would pose a "long-term" problem for you. To those who want to believe but can't bring their minds and hearts to that state, Pascal recommends to live as if one believed and then belief may come. If we want that prize, then we must wager accordingly. How best to live, in order to foster this belief?

BE MERCIFUL, AS YOUR HEAVENLY FATHER IS...

Although made in God's image and likeness, our sinful imperfections damage our relationships with him and with each other. If we are stuck on justice then belief can become dry, weak and fragile As the Hebrew Scriptures attest with Abraham, Moses and Noah, God never tires in his offer of covenants to every one of his creatures, no matter how often we break them, because of his infinite love for us. For it is through God's desire that that relationship is restored, and is enabled through his gift of *mercy*. Can we do the same, and then teach our children to do likewise?

In his epic ode, "The Hound of Heaven," Francis Thompson's lyrics describe his efforts to elude a relentlessly pursuing God, so that despite the anguish of his lifestyle he could continue *his* pursuit of the addictive pleasures that would ultimately lead him to homelessness and an attempt at suicide:

> "I fled Him, down the nights and down the days;
> I fled Him, down the arches of the years;
> I fled Him, down the labyrinthine ways
> Of my own mind; and in the midst of tears"

Thompson's verse reminds us of similar efforts by Augustine, as both believed yielding to God's entreaties of unbounded love would mean abandoning worldly delights—the only gratifications each seemed to know. But writing as if he were the observer of this chase, Thompson allows God to speak through him, and appeal to him, proclaiming the love that surpasses all despite the depths to which one has sunk:

> How little worthy of any love thou art!
> Whom wilt thou find to love ignoble thee,
> ....Save Me, save only Me?
> All which I took from thee, I did but take,
> ....Not for thy harms,
> But just that thou might'st seek it in My arms.
> ....All which thy child's mistake,
> Fancies as lost, I have stored for thee at home:
> ....Rise, clasp My hand, and come."

Rather than a depressing tale of tragedy, Thompson's story glorifies the triumph of faith stemming from the mercy and charity he received from his rescuers, and then ultimately gave back to them.

During the times in my adult life when I thought I had been badly wronged, forgiveness was the furthest thought from my mind; and when the idea would intrude upon me, it was quickly pushed aside by a bad memory. That pattern repeated itself, until one day I began to sense some distant and vague promptings whose origins were unknown to me. Were these faint impulses the distant baying from *my* "Hound of heaven?" If so, what exactly was the Hound saying? The impulses had been intermittently intruding into my thoughts, and listening more closely I heard the whisper: "*forgiveness.*"

Eventually, during one recitation of the greatest prayer taught by Jesus to his disciples, I began to wonder how many times I had only given lip service, and agreed to forgive those who had hurt me only after first petitioning to *receive* forgiveness for whom I had hurt? Too many to count, or ignore. I knew what my faith taught; but I also knew how inconsistent I was living it. Earlier in my life, the problem I had was thinking that forgiveness was contingent upon a change in one's feelings; but I learned that that change is not necessary, although much more likely with repentance. And when both occur, so, too, can transformation and, ideally, reconciliation.

In time I understood that forgiveness, like our virtues, was an act of one's free will. As with any aspect of life, one could overrule one's feelings by making a choice to do the right thing—however difficult that choice initially was. This understanding, and the subsequent right decision, required many conversations with God. Occasionally, my part of those discussions veered toward argument; but each time my Irish reared up my conscience reared even higher, helping me to acknowledge—quite uncomfortably—my own need for "*forgive us our trespasses...*" I needed to be transformed so that I could be able to transcend the difficult challenge posed by the act of forgiving, and perceive a greater understanding of what waited for me beyond that charitable act. Notwithstanding his breathtaking miracles and the divinity behind them, Jesus' greatest virtue was his unlimited capacity for being loving and merciful, and offering the forgiveness and healing they wrought. And he asks his followers, those who purport to be *Christ-like* (*Christian*), to do the same. It can seem impossible, when *our* emotions and intellect are in charge; but if we use our free will to allow *His* will to work through us, then forgiveness can surely happen.

In Shakespeare's *The Merchant of Venice*, Shylock rightly seeks justice from the Venetian courts because of the great debt owed to him by Antonio. Portia, however, recommends that he show mercy to his merchant client. When Shylock resists, and insists upon his "pound of flesh" if not money, Portia reinforces the greater value of mercy in her dramatic courtroom speech. It makes a striking contrast to the harsh justice sought by the Jewish moneylender, and seems to be the English bard's way of encouraging the Christian virtue in his time, and perhaps beyond:

> The quality of mercy is not strain'd,
> It droppeth as the gentle rain from heaven
> Upon the place beneath: it is twice blest;
> It blesseth him that gives and him that takes:

Going further in a role that suggests Lady Wisdom (for a time), Portia reminds Shylock of the consequences to all who rely solely on the slow wheels of justice—in God's law or Man's—because their slow turn "grinds fine,"

> Though justice be thy plea, consider this:
> That in the course of justice none of us
> Should see salvation. We do pray for mercy,
> And that same prayer doth teach us all to render
> The deeds of mercy

Portia knew we need justice, but much more mercy.

Throughout my life, I, too, have deserved justice for my sins, and have received it. But in each case I ultimately received mercy because, like the Prodigal Son, I turned toward its source—the Merciful Father. And my testimony has been preceded countless times, as evidenced by the fact that every book within the Bible has a merciful theme, none more than in the Gospels.

A dramatically profound and moving example of this unfolds in the Fourth Gospel, when Jesus is said to be teaching in the Temple courtyard during the Feast of the Tabernacles, a celebration of God's generous provision of the Jewish people during their 40-year exile in the Wilderness. The Lord is about to provide for them, and us, yet again.

As the feast was winding down on its final day, the religious elders presented to Jesus a woman who had been caught in adultery. Referring to him as "Teacher," they purport a respect that was merely a façade because they had no history of such deference to him, and they had been plotting ways to kill him. So their interest in the woman's crime was secondary, since their primary motivation was to use her as bait in order to trick Jesus into condemning himself. The elders knew that if he recommended leniency for this sinner, then he would be condemned for failing to uphold the punishing Law of Moses; but if he condemned her, then her public humiliation would have been complete with her stoning. That outcome would have resulted in those hypocritical leaders being seen as righteous, in contrast with Jesus, despite their immoral conduct. Part of that immorality was their accusation of *only* the woman, when the Mosaic Law requires that *both* parties be brought for trial. Jesus must have known this, since he was a teacher of the law, so he would have known how unjustly the law was being applied toward her. His sympathy and respect for her was in line with his similar behavior toward other women, including Martha and Mary, at the death of Lazarus, Mary Magdalene, at Jesus' resurrection, and the Samaritan woman at the well.

As the crowd of men grew agitated and gripped their stones, Jesus remained on the ground and began to write with his finger in the dirt. We do not know what those tracings meant; but perhaps they were a fulfillment of Jeremiah 17:13, in which the prophet writes, "…they that depart from me shall be written in the earth, because they have forsaken the Lord." Is that a warning to those who act immorally as part of their rejection of him, indicating that they condemn *themselves* by their actions? In an earlier Temple experience, Jesus had demonstrated his willingness to flip the tables of hypocrites and evildoers. But in this case he flipped the plans of the hypocritical leaders, by instructing any among them to cast their weapon *only* if they were without sin. This brilliant strategy placed the burden of both the sentencing and execution on those elders rather than on him. The maneuver seems to have also caused some introspection and guilt, since all of them dropped their weapon and walked away. This may be seen as self-condemnation; but perhaps it was the first step toward their salvation—because Jesus came for all.

I imagine that all who have ever encountered the will and mercy of Jesus must have reacted, at least momentarily, in stunned silence, overwhelmed, as they would have been, by the love they had just experienced. The silence of this woman makes it seem reasonable to conclude that she had more than just a moment of that reaction. In the quiet that ensued she probably just stared at her defender, a man unlike any other and one whose hands held no stones. When Jesus "straightened up," as John tells us, and asked if any accusers remained to condemn her, I imagine the woman's startled reaction delayed her reply, at which point she could muster only a whisper, "No one, sir." To that Jesus replied with a reassurance that all humanity hopes to hear, and then a declaration that most today seem to ignore, "Neither do I condemn you." Go, and *sin no more*." God is mercy, but only because of sin.

God is Love, but also More…

While many of today's believers in God see him as love in the form of only a noun, it is more accurate to understand him as both noun *and* verb. This improvement is indicated by the *acting* love described earlier by our charity toward each other. During my theology program, Dr. Joseph Gower repeatedly emphasized the point that "God is love loving," meaning that his love is both in his being *and* his doing. Without his action of giving love, of loving us, we could never receive it, thereby making any admiration of his love, or belief in it, as pointless as any admiration we would have for a physician who, despite having the highest academic credentials, never uses his craft in order to help anyone. He *is* but never *does*. The esteem would not last long because we not only exist, we *do*. And we would therefore look elsewhere for help—and truth.

So love is not meant to be kept, but to be given; otherwise, it has no value. And therein lies the great source of our dignity. While God loves all his creation, he loves us most of all because we were given his image and likeness. To many, "image" would seem to be enough, but the addition of the synonymous "likeness" is a Hebrew way of adding emphasis to our relationship to God. And because he is the source of all intelligence, we are creations bestowed with reason whose intellectual freedom can receive his love and return it, and whose free will can also reject it. Love would not be possible had we been made robots, or as Pavlovian beings. We needed to be created so we could be the recipients of his love, and freely choose to be in a relationship with him.

Our experience of that love urges us to give testimony as witnesses by sharing it with others. Important as they are to the continued understanding and growth of Christianity, profound theological explanations were not the main reasons faith spread from one man to twelve, and then to billions of men, women, and children. Nor are they the reasons for the vast number of Christian charities such as hospitals, schools, and orphanages. And finally, they are not the reasons people have given up their lives—and still do—for their love of something and someone other than themselves.

No, it was the "greater love" exemplified by Jesus of Nazareth—a charitable love that offers a transformative relationship, one that resulted in those twelve followers and the subsequent billions. To deny all this, in the agnostic or atheistic fashion of the day, is to conclude that billions of reasonable people fell for either a lunatic or fraud, as proposed by C. S. Lewis. And this denial defies the factual logic, reality and truth of the cosmos, one that, according to Cardinal Joseph Ratzinger (later, Pope Benedict XVI), necessarily "leads to the conclusion of the existence of a great intelligence, which has thought the world into being." Jesus the Christ is the ultimate reality of all creation, and the Word that begat creation. It is a great curiosity that disbelief occurs simultaneously with belief in the existence of many ancient historical figures, despite the larger amount of documentation (including non-biblical records that include Tacitus, Josephus and Pliny the Younger) attesting to the existence, deeds and crucifixion of Jesus—and to the truth in the Gospels. The greatest love occurred in Jesus' death, while victory over that death is the enigma of Easter: Jesus' apparent defeat results in the greatest of victories. Now *that's* transformation.

So this is the faith that Kevin, Maureen, and I affirm with both heart and head, and one that we must know and live—in charity—to fulfill our collective destiny. The knowledge of our dignity and subsequent worth from being sought after by our Creator is a powerful truth; and it is this seeking, along with the beliefs that grow out of it and the charity that springs from it, that offers us the opportunity to go through and beyond our challenges—to flourish in a life of fulfillment.

CHAPTER 15

The Transcendent More

Because of his anguish he shall see the light; because of his knowledge he shall be content.

—Isaiah 53:10

"I wish it need not have happened in my time," said Frodo. "So do I," said Gandalf, "and so do all who live to see such times. But that is not for them to decide. All we have to decide is what to do with the time that is given us."
"The Fellowship of the Ring"

J.R.R. Tolkien

CHILDHOOD SHOULD BE A TIME of certainty, especially for the fortunate families not struggling with poverty, war and famine, but too often it is not. And when children suddenly become less certain, especially from struggles within the family, the normal challenges of their journey become more difficult. That is a scandal crying out for justice, and one so compelling that Jesus warned us of the severest consequences to those causing "the little ones" to lose their way.

Despite the uncertainties of our new family, I never doubted we would see our way through because of the love we shared. We were united in a "herculean knot" of love, a love Thomas More described having had with his children. This love would help bring to fruition the hope in these lines from Wordsworth:

> Though nothing can bring back the hour
> Of splendor in the grass, of glory in the flower;
> We will grieve not, rather find
> Strength in what remains behind.

We did, however, grieve at the change. We also felt the frustration at times, as if we were fighting our way through thick pudding but getting nowhere while making a mess. But we eventually looked purposefully for the strength each had in the love and trust we shared.

Turning the Corner

As close as my children and I were prior to this period, the next few years brought us that much closer—by necessity and by our intentions. We became a bit stoical in the face of some difficulties, and eventually found we could return humor to our daily lives. We learned that despite troubles of *any* kind, we could choose our responses. One option would be to claim the mantle of "victim," in an effort to excuse poor behavior. But the better option would be to see problems differently than they first appeared, and then persevere while figuring out a way to gain something good out of it—eventually to encourage others. However, we must also not let that define our lives, or discourage us in future relationships.

During my earlier professional life I was director of a rehabilitation program for those with heart disease. Most of the participants had suffered heart attacks, and subsequently defined themselves by their disease—sometimes crippling themselves emotionally. In reflecting back on those experiences, I saw a valuable comparison to the advice I was giving to my children, and to myself, about not identifying ourselves with any of our travails. The heart program participants were encouraged to accept the new reality that had been forced upon them, which is that part of their heart's function was permanently diseased. In an effort to come to terms with this new status, participants were taught to broaden both the meaning and opportunities of their new reality. Patients were taught to tip their hats at the trouble they were passing through, and then explore ways of realizing a fuller meaning and potential for the remainder of their heart—and their lives. Not all patients learned these lessons well, and risked becoming "cardiac cripples;" because although their cardiovascular system recovered, their mental, emotional and spiritual "systems" did not.

Joseph Campbell wrote that the road of trials is "a series of tests, tasks, and ordeals that the person must undergo to begin the transformation" into heroism. He views this aspect of the journey "as a favorite phase of the myth-adventure," presumably in part because of the epic battle, but mostly because overcoming these great ordeals has given us the legends to model. However, as we read these stories and the fascinating accounts in history books and novels, it is worth remembering that the forging of that heroism was frequently a response to pain and tragedy, and sometimes without justice—at least during the hero's earthly life. Still, their transformation of both the challenges *and* themselves encourages us to do likewise with our difficulties—helping us to overcome and then take our turn to become models for others. That, again, is the power of giving witness—it benefits the *other* in our lives.

Can we affirm having had a good life, even a wonderful life, despite it not having been free from great difficulties? It seems impossible to have a life free of travails. Heroism, in fact, owes its existence to our challenges. So our good lives will necessarily be the result of a triumphant life, committing to overcome our struggles—including those that are self-inflicted—and "carry on," as Robert Service said, to the successful completion of our journey and fulfillment of our purpose. That never means pretending one's troubles do not exist, because that would be dishonest and not a credible model to others. More than that, it would deny us the truth of our own history and the lessons we continue to learn from it.

But how best to get through life's big trials, and come out the other side to live a flourishing *eudaimonia*, a blessed and happy life? We don't typically have an obvious preparation for these specific challenges. And why should we? It is one thing to prepare children for, say, bullies at school, but it is ludicrous to think parents would begin preparing children for inevitable travails at home or horrors outside it. So we hope, but on what basis? For some of us, it is simply the fleeting wishes of positive thinking, or a "keep your fingers crossed" type of hope that is unattached to a meaningful foundation of moral conviction. That conviction is found in Jesus' greatest sermon on how to live a flourishing and fulfilled life, because the supreme happiness pledged at the beginning of each of the Beatitudes results in the hope promised at their conclusions. For others of us, any attempt at "keeping the faith" is made difficult because that faith resides only in us—flawed creatures that we are. But for those successful along their journey, something else must be behind the faith and hope that enabled them to experience that blessed happiness, and rise above the demons they encountered. So, what is it?

In his letter to the fractious Jewish and Gentile believers within the city of Corinth, Saint Paul addresses a fledgling church struggling because of a variety of immoral behaviors among its members. He lays blame at the feet of pride and selfishness, two spirits that have haunted the human race since shortly after its origin, and then launches into what is perhaps his most famous moral instruction, one echoed throughout countless weddings—including my own. The apostle acknowledges the importance of the three Godly virtues, but makes clear the emptiness of faith and barrenness of hope when *love* is not present: "If I have all faith so as to move mountains, but have not love, I am nothing." That is why he concluded his great teaching by saying, "...the greatest of these is love." This particular love is divine. It is the transcendent and yet imminent charity that originates with God, which we then give freely to others. It is the agape love described earlier, and the way we realize true happiness.

For many, a trial can be overwhelming and incomprehensible, such that they are consumed by it. They see nothing else. This is especially true for young children, because they haven't been fully formed and can't imagine transcendence. But if along the way their faith and hope have been formed from or buoyed by an unconditional love, then they have a foundation of self-worth, dignity and the sacred upon which to imagine life beyond their difficulties..

These challenges make me recall a particular scene in *The Yearling*, a novel by Marjorie Kinnan Rawlings, about a twelve-year-old boy's struggle to find his way in the harsh and lonesome frontier, and to become a *man*. Jody and his father have a particularly close relationship, but it was put to a severe test by the tragic circumstances surrounding the death of a young deer that he had grown to love.

Returning home after having run away during the conflict, he has a touching reunion with his family brought on by forgiveness. It is then he hears these sober and heartfelt words, reflecting the love and wisdom of his pioneer father despite their lack of refinement:

> "You've seed how things goes in the world o' men…Ever' man wants life to be a fine thing, and a easy. 'Tis fine, boy, powerful fine, but 'tain't easy. Life knocks a man down and he gits up and it knocks him down agin. A man's heart aches, seein' his young uns face the world. Knowin' they got to get their guts tore out, the way his was tore. I wanted to spare you, long as I could. I wanted you to frolic with your yearlin'. I knowed the lonesomeness he eased for you. But ever' man's lonesome. What's he to do then? What's he to do when he gits knocked down? Why, take it for his share and go on."

Jody does take it and goes on, maturing from this experience and the subsequent triumphs and tragedies he would eventually face.

In *The Lord of the Rings*, Frodo suffers while enduring a mission he volunteered for on behalf of others, and although forever changed as the shire is, he fulfills his destiny—with the help of his fellow apostle, Samwise. During his struggle, the conflicted Boromir is most like us in his humanity, as he succumbs to the lure of the ring—the Temptress on his hero's journey. But he breaks free of the evil clutches; and upon realizing his sin he strives to overcome his corruption, exercising virtue by rescuing Merry and Pippin and then redeeming himself by making the ultimate loving sacrifice.

Not long after being shocked from the grace of forgiveness by Bishop Myriel, for stealing the bishop's silver cutlery, escaped convict Jean Valjean reduces a 12-year-old boy to tears by stealing *his* silver coin. Stunned at realizing the depths to which his soul has descended, Valjean collapses in racking sobs and cries out, "I'm such a miserable man!" This acknowledgment is the beginning of his conversion to a life of great charity, culminating with its complete transformation by the great gift of his life for others.

Toward the end of "The Adventure of the Veiled Lodger," a story involving the tragic circumstances of a horribly disfigured woman, Sherlock Holmes announces the case is closed. The woman acknowledges him, but in a voice that instantly alarms the detective. He turns abruptly to her, and exclaims, "Your life is not your own! Keep your hands off it!" When the poor woman questions Holmes about the merits of continuing on rather than ending her suffering, he replies, "How can you tell? The example of patient suffering is in itself the most precious of all lessons to an impatient world." Two days later Holmes received in the mail from the lodger a bottle containing prussic acid, or cyanide, testimony to the life-affirming choice the woman made. Her suffering is particularly noble, for it is in service as a lesson to those whom she would never know and from whom she would hear no gratitude.

These stories teach us that glory comes from persevering in virtue for the sake of ourselves *and others*, whereby we emerge from our ordeals changed either as models to be emulated or, if vanquished, legends to be acclaimed. They describe a suffering Aristotle would call "pathos," of a kind that could prevent someone from living a full life or a happy life—if one allows it, or if one cannot see more than their suffering or more than they are at that present time. But, as described earlier, the happiness of which he spoke pertained to our "flourishing," and not the sentimental emotion of our current time. In the same way our Greek ancestors eloquently helped us to understand *love* more fully, they did so with their words for "happiness," as mentioned earlier. Yet there is an even greater state of happiness, or divine bliss, than *eudaimonia*, one that is the highest form of that virtuous life.

Makarios is the "supremely blessed" moral state that exists independent of one's situation or how one feels. It is the running theme of those Beatitudes, the greatest guide to living virtuously and emblematic of the three theological virtues: *faith, hope* and *love*. And the highest virtue within those teachings, and within that Teacher, is the *agape* love of God. The joy that comes from this love, despite what comes from life, means they could have been written, "*Happy* are the virtuous heroes…*for how they transform themselves, their troubles and others.*"

THOMAS MORE AND VIKTOR FRANKL

In good marriages, husband and wife share the *eudaimonia* and perhaps *makarios* amidst the burden of each other's struggles. This is the blessing of marriage, and one that both Thomas More and psychiatrist Viktor Frankl experienced. More, during the time leading up to his arrest and throughout his imprisonment in the Tower of London, had the support and devotion, if not always the quiet comfort, of his voluble wife, Alice. Frankl, writing in *Man's Search for Meaning*, described frequent thoughts of his wife as one reason for his survival during the nightmare years in a German concentration camp. Those who do not know these men would understandably conclude that the important thread each shared, that allowed him to bravely face his respective struggle, was having a good wife. This conclusion could discourage those without such a wife. However, further contemplation of More and Frankl made me see that this thread was only part of a larger fabric—and not the major part.

As their respective trials unfolded, both men suffered greatly, with Thomas More paying the ultimate price and Frankl witnessing the same fate of his loved ones. Neither of them ignored the reality, or attempted a false optimism, because either decision would have proven harmful and resulted in despair. Instead, both came to realize the freedom they had. But unlike the delusional freedom noted elsewhere in this book, which asserts a reality having no basis in fact and no direction toward truth, each came to terms with the reality of their situation—however harsh—and discovered the freedom to recognize a twofold truth of his existence that went far beyond his body, his circumstance, and his wife.

The first truth is that each of us can decide to follow Aristotle's instruction, and explore the depths of our struggles and find a greater meaning of those experiences—perhaps a greatness—which, while not initially apparent, is always present in wait of discovery and that cannot not be taken away. Rather than just immersing ourselves in the *feelings* of pain, sorrow, loneliness, etc., we can use our *reason*, *will* and *imagination* to move our way through and then beyond these feelings and, more importantly, their causes, in a way that helps us have greater understanding and gives those experiences different meaning.

The second truth is that the greatest meaning we could ultimately find from that reasoning and imagining, is love—of one's faith, a profound memory, or most especially, a person or persons. Frankl described this ability as having the "capacity for self-transcendence" in any trial, allowing us to first go beyond ourselves and then realize we are part of something much more meaningful than any particular circumstance. For Frankl, this was faith as well as reason, because the ultimate manifestation of this is a somewhat comprehensible "Supermeaning," he noted, one corresponding to "a Superbeing we would call God."

Had Frankl been trained in Christian doctrine as had More, he would have understood this "larger" or "ultimate" reality to be the *grace* described in earlier chapters, a gift from the Superbeing that eagerly awaits our acceptance. Notwithstanding the many entreaties made of More that he accede to the King's command (including desperate ones from his beloved daughter), the formation of his conscience led him to the conviction that he had only one path, come what may—and that path is known, traditionally, as "truth." That is, More knew he could not support the lies behind his king's plans to be the head of the breakaway Catholic Church in England, and to seek annulment of his first marriage so he could then remarry. His loyalty was to the true pope and the true marriage, a virtue borne from a well-formed conscience.

Transcending the Suffering

When dealing with suffering along our journey, Aristotle's suggestion is to respond by finding some joy in the difficult experience, as this translation indicates: "Suffering becomes beautiful when anyone bears great calamities with cheerfulness, not through insensibility (i.e., pretending one has no trouble) but through greatness of mind." This forbearance would seem to fly in the face of the deconstructed masculinity being taught in our schools. But questions persist, about how one can develop this mind and its potential for heroism. Those questions are legitimate, since Aristotle also believed that certain suffering could overwhelm our minds and our senses, thereby preventing our ability to recover from them. Perhaps he was right, especially if most people could not easily develop such a mind as the philosopher recommended. And would that limitation of philosophy be its complexity in helping us understand our struggles, let alone transcend them in order to look back and reinterpret them? I think so. But what if Aristotle wasn't right?

The world in which the Athenian philosopher lived hadn't yet been impacted by the one who said, "Behold, I make all things new." The ancient Greeks had no god who wanted to become fully human, nor one who had lived with them and sacrificed his or her life for them; nor, especially, one who resurrected to an eternal *makarios*—and then offered the same destiny to them. As theologian Fr. Michael Himes notes in *The Mystery of Faith*, "The Incarnation," that is, God *desiring* to become human, "is the highest compliment ever paid to being human." God wanted to be one of us, as both a sublime reality and transcendent truth, and did so in the *divine person* of Jesus the Christ and in the concrete reality of this same person who took on the *human nature* of Jesus of Nazareth.

Even if one believed that last part to be only a fable, or a pure mythology absent any kernel of truth, the historical facts of Jesus and, especially, his ministry and crucifixion, point to a goodness that would be the greatest example for us to emulate. Why? Because "greater love has no man, than that he lay down his life for his friends." And both the love in his death and the hope in his resurrection give us the greatest examples of transforming the meaning of the suffering experience, to something much, much greater than it seems in its moments. Perhaps the final choice by that veiled lodger, the heroism she displayed, is an example of *makarios* and her recognition of her inherent dignity. But the will of Jesus, to both submit to the crucifixion and then will the resurrection, *is makarios* personified.

The Persevering Spirit

Throughout the remainder of our hero's journey we must decide to persevere through the inevitable obstacles, receiving help from others *and* helping others to overcome. Ultimately, we can rejoice in the willed transformation of our circumstances and ourselves, and in the knowledge that our dignity is only enhanced by that change. We must model past and current heroes, and be taught to uncover the truth of a greater meaning that that conversion offers. We must be the example that encourages others around us, as well as those who will certainly follow. By making these choices we will not remain with Plato's unknowing cave dwellers, but will instead be transformed by the light of truth that awaits the seeker. And by our actions and the legacy they leave, many will realize the transformative joy that so much of life holds for those willing to take the hero's journey. Having done this, we flourish as our potential suggests and our destiny confirms; and we end our passage not as the lonesome hero riding off into the sunset, but as part of a *community* of heroes sharing the celebration.

I emphasize the above because our culture won't teach it. Today we completely miss the *virtue* part of happiness, which is the joy and fulfillment that comes from selfless *giving*, and instead base our misunderstanding on the superficial and temporary good feelings from whatever we *get*. Many point to Jefferson's "pursuit of happiness," failing to realize how grounded his philosophy was in the *eudaimonia* and *makarios* of Socrates, Plato, Aristotle and, especially, Jesus, whose teachings he asserted provide "outlines of a system of the most sublime morality which has ever fallen from the lips of man." So when the circumstances change, as they inevitably will, their unmoored and sentimental happiness will be washed away—leaving them bereft of the security this understanding provides. To succeed along the hero journey, one must give in order to be fulfilled and, ultimately, blessed.

This potential heroism is the spirit that lies within all, compelling us to go on and give of ourselves to those in need when the apparent reality makes that seem very difficult, if not impossible. It is a powerful mystery, that despite suffering from the traumas of life, from the "attacks of the heart" caused by us or by others, these very same hearts can rally and act virtuously because of their inexhaustible supply of love, and the perpetual freedom to choose this love. In some ways, the easy part is recognizing the freedom each of us has; but the harder part is then choosing the most moral virtue, despite how we feel. For feelings, like hunger, come and go, but love of the deepest kind is permanent. These are our selfless loves that are deeply committed to the well-being of the other. They are our heroic loves—the love I have for Kevin and Maureen.

During one afternoon in early 2008, shortly after the divorce, Maureen demonstrated the highest love for me as well as the transformation within her, when her simple but profound gesture wiped away the winter doldrums. She and I were in the study going through the computer files, when she came upon a folder of mine labeled "poems." When my daughter asked about them I winced a bit, before replying that almost all were related to the family that was. She turned briefly away, and then suddenly turned back to me with conviction ablaze in her blue eyes and said, "Then make one for me." The strength of her reply did not mask the tenderness and love within it, a combination that proved very moving and made my spirits soar.

The resultant exchange of her spoken love with mine, that I later wrote into verse, made me think of the many exchanges between Thomas More and his daughter Margaret, letters that made clear the most profound love the two shared. I'm not sure my poem did justice to her request, bringing to mind More's reply to another of Margaret's loving letters to him while he languished in prison, "your daughterly loving letter, my dearly beloved child, was and is, I faithfully assure you, much more inward comfort unto me than my pen can well express you." Maureen truly is my "dearly beloved" daughter.

If I were asked which impressed me more about Maureen's words—her strength of character or her desire to lift my spirits—I would say it didn't matter. That is because the love behind both made me eager to write it and give thanks for a daughter who thought enough of her father to want to honor him this way.

The culminating act of charity for Kevin occurred while he was a senior and Maureen a freshman in the same high school, during the final wrestling match of his school career. Part of this "senior night" tradition has each wrestler on the team meet a family member on the mat, giving a token gift if appropriate. I was not sure how we would handle this.

The festivities began with a speech by the coach, after which the presentations commenced. The athletes were introduced in order of their weight class, with the lightest going first. As the wrestler before Kevin was leaving the mat, Maureen and I rose from the bleachers to make our way down to the mat, not knowing what to expect. But just at that moment Kevin surprised everyone when he suddenly grabbed some flowers that were nearby, and then bolted from the mat toward the bleachers and us. We stopped in confusion, but after realizing his plan I turned and went back to my seat while Maureen remained. He made a determined zigzag pattern up through the spectators, protecting his gift while his eyes remained focused on his path. The delicate floral bouquet grabbed by Kevin framed a powerful contrast, as they were in the hands of one who would soon use those very same hands in furious combat. As he released his grip on the bouquet to the gentle, welcoming hand of his adoring sister, Maureen's face beamed with the love they have always shared.

Despite our uniqueness, Kevin, Maureen and I have many similarities, and among them are our imperfections. But while the flaws from poor judgment are the worst kind, they also offer the greatest opportunity for humility, empathy and, ultimately, charity. When boys combine these virtues with the toughness forged by trials, manhood truly is in the making. Kevin's test, unlike the test for the young Masai warrior, was not to slay a lion. And it wasn't even to defeat his wrestling opponent. Instead, it was to echo both More and Frankl by making a free-will choice to persevere through a trial not of his doing, to know the eternal love of his family and seek the fuller truth of this life to benefit himself and others. When we do this, we transcend our dilemma, have hope, and then move to something greater—and better. By his actions, he gave virtue to his life, honor to his father and sister, and witness to others about an important step in a heroic journey.

Kevin and Maureen helped me to transform potentially difficult experiences into ones filled with joy, making sacred acts of unforgettable charity whose effects will forever unfold.

Boys are heroes-in-waiting. Some wait eagerly, others desperately, in the hope that a good man will care enough to take responsibility for loving them and teaching them the necessary virtues. If that happens, then those boys, too, can take their position among the pantheon of heroes, and do the same.

Men have a simple choice. And whatever we choose will be our legacy long after we're gone, be it for good or ill. History will allow future generations to look back on us, either to point the finger of blame or raise a glass in praise. Doing the right thing is simple, but often not easy. If we have erred, no matter how many times, then we should make amends before it is too late. As Viktor Frankl said, "Everything can be taken from a man but…the last of the human freedoms—to choose one's attitude in any given set of circumstances, to choose one's own way." As a Christian, I would only add, "to choose the truth of Christ," because that is the permanent standard against which all our actions should be measured.

Heroism must always be prepared and at the ready, but not as boastful machismo that masks a deep uncertainty. Instead, as a boy moves into manhood, he must learn that his virtuous character exemplifies manliness. Thomas More exemplified this trait, because despite a failing body and aching heart, he chose to face the great moral dilemma of saving his life for a lie rather than losing it for the truth—and chose the latter because of a well-formed conscience. Although his journey was cut short, his heroism lives on. While most boys will never be tested to that extent, they will be tested, repeatedly, no matter the season of life. So they should therefore strive to become like More, formed to be steadfast to the truth of their convictions no matter the circumstances they face. Behaving as such, each will have earned the respect from his contemporaries as More did, and the perpetual honor that More has, as being "a man for all seasons."

POSTLUDE

NOTWITHSTANDING THE DIFFICULTIES, I HAVE been blessed with two versions of a happy family. Each of us must seek God's purpose in our lives, and then find the mission to fulfill it, as a blessed outcome is well worth the risk of the necessary efforts. Had I not assumed that risk, I would have known neither the greatest marital love nor the two greatest blessings and joys in my life. While the book records stories about us, each is only used to illustrate points that are much more than us. And while that "more" pertains mostly to the formation of boys into manhood, many pertain to girls as well. So it is important for the reader to know that while stories about both my son and boys predominate over those involving Maureen and girls, both my darling daughter and girls in general are no less important to me. Everyone matters.

While involving the range of emotions, the stories ultimately tell of an overarching joy in the fullest sense of that word from the transforming actions described in each. I'm filled with gratitude that we have had the good fortune to realize this joy; and I'll leave to others the determination of how valuable my contribution was to that experience. Yet I know that in this life, too many children have never had these experiences, due in large part to their broken hearts. But the grounded hope described earlier, and not naïve optimism, truly springs eternal.

The various iterations of this book have taken several years to write, involving many frustrations and blessings along the way. Each version was due to significant changes—mostly in me—and the providential enlightenment they provided. The outcome of our efforts is known only to a power that is both in and beyond this world. But as I close this book I will remain secure in my belief that virtue can accompany us to the successful conclusion of our hero's journey, if we but *will* it.

IN GRATITUDE

To JOE, PAUL, MARTY, CHRISTINE, Linda, Carolyn and Claire, loving siblings who were instrumental in my formation—for good or ill!

To my friends and mentors, in order of appearance in my life. Some helped Kevin's formation, and all helped mine—even if we do not always agree:

Chris Tivenan, the Alpha and Omega of friendship, from first grade onward; Gerry Tivenan, a beloved father figure, whose premature passing saddened me but gladdened the hearts in Heaven; Remo D. Maisto, the Roman Paisan; Steve Freedman, my rock-solid Hebrew mensch with whom humor is always on standby; Mark Occhipinti, stalwart friend with a chest big enough to hold his large heart; Ralph de St Aubin, my "left" handed doctor whose best medicine comes *not* from his black bag; Phil Keane, neighbor-friend who never wavered; Ken Small, my "Show-me state" friend who, with his devoted wife, picked up everything and drove over eleven-hundred miles to help me—Semper Fi; Reverend James Occhipinti, ("Pastor O") with the unshakable faith of an Old Testament prophet; Monsignor Ken Tuzeneu, for the past decade a faithful lodestar for my children and me, so important to my renewal; Dan Duddy, a "Daniel" whose bold faith has helped him courageously fight off many lions, within and without, and which has given him a wonderful story to tell. I know some of that story, and the faith of the man behind it; so I can't wait to read it; Steven Lento, my first editor, whose blunt challenges forced me to reexamine my positions so that I could properly defend them—or abandon them; Janis Hutchinson, my next editor and esteemed mentor, who brilliantly reworked and organized the most challenging chapters, while providing the wisest counsel; my faithful brothers in "That Man Is You!" especially Danny, Donald, Ed, Rob and Vinnie (I commit to becoming manlier with that @#$%^&*() remote!) and "Bagel and Bible;" theologian Dr. Joseph Gower, professor of theology at Georgian Court University, mentor and friend, whose Socratic classrooms and office discussions made me imagine my theology degree experience as redolent of the ancient "Academy," something I never thought I would experience and for which I will be eternally grateful. Whether or not my ideas prevailed, I was allowed to develop them and express them—because there were no safe spaces. This resulted in a richer faith, deeper understanding and a better man. His review of key chapters was profoundly helpful, and any flaws in them are due to his student's limitations. This, too, was essential to my renewal; my GCU classmates, Mike McKenna, Paul Addo and Kathleen Brady (she agrees with me more than she'll admit). I hesitated going into the program, but their camaraderie, faithfulness and humor make me all the more thankful for such a wonderful experience; Dana Seiden, my final editor, whose opening comment sparked an essential change in my thinking, and in the book; Robert Bolt, and the inspiration received from both the contents and title of his most successful play, "A Man for All Seasons"; Professor Rhonda Clements, for the courtesy and kindness of reviewing the manuscript, and her subsequent encouragement; Kevin and Maureen, for their critical review of key chapters (they know that although they contributed to it, the book isn't about them—for which they are glad!); and, the many men and women who gave witness and, especially, their lives, in order that my children and I would know the truth behind the Faith we share, a faith that teaches us to endure and flourish—with others. Finally, it is the *Patri et Filii et Spiritus Sancti* that taught me the most about love and family.

ABOUT THE AUTHOR

THOMAS CAFFREY RUNS AN INJURY management business while building a web-based ministry (www.faithpilgrims.com). He works in several men's faith formation ministries, and recently earned a MA Theology degree from Georgian Court University. He has been writing for 25 years, and his poem on John Adams earned First Place in C-SPAN's "American Presidents" series of 2000. He lives on the Jersey Shore with his large gardens, larger imagination, and children.

www.ingramcontent.com/pod-product-compliance
Lightning Source LLC
Chambersburg PA
CBHW060517100426
42743CB00009B/1345